Memories of COWICHAN LAKE

A Life at Greendale

TREVOR GREEN • TONY GREEN • LEXI BAINAS

Tellwell Talent
www.tellwell.ca

ISBN
978-0-2288-3479-3 (Hardcover)
978-0-2288-3478-6 (Paperback)
978-0-2288-3480-9 (eBook)

About the Author

The author of this book (Trevor Green) was born in Duncan on Sept. 14, 1912. At the age of three or four, he was running around his home and his father's small farm trying to be of help.

As he grew older he collected and washed eggs and was in charge of the many chickens and pigeons and as he grew older he looked after the cows, goats, and horses.

Trevor went to school in Lake Cowichan with 11 other students ranging in age from six to 13. Grades nine to 12 he spent in Victoria as there was no high school in either Lake Cowichan or Duncan. In Victoria he stayed with his father's sisters for more than three years until his high school education was completed. He got to know Victoria very well, cycling around a lot after school and on weekends.

When high school was completed he returned to Greendale, the family home on the Cowichan River, and was obliged to deliver eggs, roasting chickens, milk, and fruit when it became ripe in the early fall. He did this for two or three years and then got a job at Gordon Stores, where he remained until 1963, when he finally quit, after enduring several difficult months in which his increasingly erratic employer only paid him in food.

In January 1964 Lake Cowichan High School burned almost to the ground but a few rooms were saved. Trevor managed to get the job of night watchman, which he truly enjoyed as it was a union position that paid more than twice as much as he had received at Gordon Stores. In addition, the room he got to use when not on patrol boasted a space heater, which really warmed up the place. As an added treat, there was a piano in the room so he could play for hours each night when not involved in writing his stories.

His watchman job lasted more than a year while the school was being rebuilt. Once that was finished, he was hired to create the huge playing field, which is still in use today. Part of that work included spending hour after hour raking all the rocks from the chosen ground. This job lasted six months or so and he had the pleasure of seeding it all by hand and watching eagerly as it slowly turned green.

He was not unemployed for long, and soon found a job at the Forestry Station at Mesachie Lake. He worked there until retirement at age 65. After that he was employed as watchman, which entailed watering all the seedlings and recording the weather information that was sent to the newspapers and TV in Victoria every Saturday and Sunday.

Away from work, Trevor's life revolved around hiking all the beautiful mountains around B.C. and Washington state. His love for the flora and fauna was truly evident and he knew or remembered the Latin names of every plant pointed out to him.

He loved working at the station and remained as watchman until he was 85.

After that Trevor spent hours in the gardens at Greendale and frequently in summer and autumn he and wife, Yvonne, travelled around the Island and B.C. in a Volkswagen camper van. After Yvonne died, age finally began to catch up with Trevor as he endured the onset of dementia.

His last years were spent at Chemainus Health Care. His daughter, Kathy, and his grandchildren were with him when he died on Feb. 12, 2009 at the age of 97.

Two things I will always remember about my father are the ways he faced increasing infirmity. He easily accepted giving up his driver's licence. The same applied to his going into the rest home in Chemainus. He said it was time and raised no objection to either, moving bravely towards the future as he had throughout his long life.

Tony Green

DEDICATION

This book is dedicated to Ian and Ann-Lee Ross, Derek and Doreen Todd, Therese Todd and Peggy Dumaine, Pat and Allison Shrieber, and Allan and Adeline Anderson and not forgetting my mother, Yvonne, and Uncle Brian and Cousin Myfanwy Spencer Pavelic. All these wonderful people are now deceased but they all played a big part in my father's life as he (my father) played in theirs.

I remember them all well: their generosity and kindness I will never forget.

Trevor Green often remarked that, after his passing, he hoped that his family would compile a book of his historical stories. Now that I'm in my early retirement years I decided to gather material and complete a book.

So I gratefully acknowledge him and offer Lexi Bainas a huge hug and big thanks for taking over the editing and dealing with people in the publishing world. Without her this publication would not have happened.

Tony Green

TABLE OF CONTENTS

PART I

Land on the River

*T*he indenture that was effected between my father, (Francis Jacob Green) and Alex Dunsmuir, (second son of Robert and Joan Dunsmuir) in June, 1887 was "duplicated" on September 10, 1889. It included a map of the 164 acres that became known ultimately as "Greendale", purchased from the E and N Railway at $1 per acre. Also included is a detailed list of the conditions applying to the transaction: the fact that the E and N Co. had the right to any minerals on the property, the use of any timber that might be required for construction of buildings connected with the railway, and the building of any necessary roads. At no time, however, were any of these conditions imposed.

So far as I know, the first building on the southern portion of the property facing the river was a small one-room log cabin with a narrow porch and a shake roof, built by my father and his two brothers, Charles and Alfred Green. Over the years, this cabin was enlarged and used by many summer visitors, and was rented at one time to a couple named Ben and Elsie Fellowes for several years.

It was demolished around 1948 or 1949, when several shreds of ancient newspaper used as insulation came to light making interesting reading. The log walls were still sound, but the flooring was badly rotted away.

I assume that the next building of interest is the old barn, by now over 100 years old, and still standing, though the roof has been replaced, and the shed to the right was recently restored.

Again, I believe that the three Green brothers and their cousin, William Swinerton, and several other early pioneers all worked on the barn gratis since this was the era when the few neighbours all helped a newcomer in need of assistance to get started.

For decades the barn has housed several horses, a succession of cows, even a few goats, and provided shelter for the Democrat carriage, the sleigh, (used during the severe winters of long ago) the plow, harrows, and other farm equipment.

With the advent of a Model "A" Ford in 1929, and the eventual conclusion of our milk business, the barn gradually became used as a garage, a toolshed, and a woodshed, but still it is an essential part of the life and times at Greendale.

I do not know what year the first stage of the old house was built, but in 1909, when my parents were married, it consisted of a three-room cottage, built of small logs, chinked with clay from the river, with bedroom, sitting-room, small kitchen, and verandah facing south. One hot summer day in 1911 my father had gone to the wood-lot across Greendale Road, leaving mother and baby Brian alone. Sometime later, she heard a suspicious crackling, only to realize that the kitchen roof was ablaze. It was of no use to call for help, since no one was within earshot. She hauled Brian outside, then dashed down to the river to fill a bucket to douse the roof since fortunately a ladder was close at hand, making several such trips, until, most fortunately, her brother-in-law (Alf Green), passing by on the road, saw the blaze, and raced in to help. Between them, the house was saved, but the small kitchen was destroyed.

After this, financed from mother's small savings, the present dining-room, pantry and kitchen were built as well as the upstairs quarters, (originally just one room with a window in the east and west gables.) And to the west of the sitting-room, a new bedroom and a small passage to the front verandah were completed. This bedroom was heated by a very small woodstove, which made it warm and comfortable during the winter months. Brother Brian and I shared this room throughout our early childhood.

The present dining-room porch was originally twice this size, but was later made smaller to admit more light to the dining-room.

And the bedroom leading from the dining-room was a later addition, made during the early 1920s, I assume.

That part of Greendale lying between the river and the E and N Railway line had been logged, I believe, before my father pre-empted the property, and to this day, it is possible to trace a few of the old skid roads, where the logs were hauled down to the river by horse team to be released downstream during flood season. Mother remembered the last log-drive during the winter of 1910-1911, then followed a hiatus until 1913, when the logs were hauled to Crofton or to Chemainus by logging-train.

The present big lawn, leading to the river, was laboriously cleared of the huge stumps and encroaching second-growth by my father, and one or sometimes two Chinese labourers. There are faded snapshots in an album depicting Gee, one of the Chinese, holding my brother. At this time, most of the debris was carefully burned, but some of the larger roots were hauled to the river's edge and piled along the shore to protect the banks from erosion.

The land to the east of the old house, being reasonably level, became the orchard, to be planted with young trees: apples, crabapples, pears, cherries, and walnuts that were purchased when the Biggerstaff Wilsons, next door and upstream, planted *their* orchard. These days, such trees as still remain would be well over 80 years of age.

What we refer to as "the cottage next door" was built in 1918, I think, as accommodation for the many guests who spent their summer seasons here. It consisted of two bedrooms opening onto a front porch facing the river; one bedroom was equipped with a small airtight heater. The other cottage (our present abode) next door was identical. Two other small cottages appeared later. One (now much altered) is on the driveway down to the former Ian Ross property, and the other, now more or less demolished, close to the kitchen of the old house, was used as quarters for the various cooks over the years.

To the south of the row of holly trees, there was in my early days a large chicken-house with a corrugated-iron roof to which had been added a small pigeon-house, including nesting-boxes where the young were hatched. We occasionally had pigeon-pie when the flock had increased, but every year there would be a raid from a hawk. It was shattering to see the panic of the poor birds as they sought refuge in all directions, but inevitably one luckless victim fell prey to the aggressor before, hours later, the survivors would return to their home base.

The two fields, one on each side of the driveway saw gradual changes as the decades passed. The one to the left, to motorists coming in from the village, had been named "The National Park" by brother Brian, and was, as I recall, a labyrinth of enormous stumps, fallen logs in various stages of decay, and much young second-growth, with bracken fern fast invading.

Many days, weeks, and months during my earlier years were spent *most* pleasurably in the National Park, for I looked on the presence of the stumps as a challenge, and was determined that by digging, blasting and burning, they would vanish from the scene. Since the soil was mostly fertile loam, this successful effort helped make the area what it is today: a fine pasture.

The other field to the right, as one drives in from the highway, was known as "The Chicken Field" since there were two small "colony houses" and a far larger one for the laying stock. At most, we raised more than 200 laying hens, purchasing 100 day-old-chicks year after year; the young cockerels were separated, of course, and fattened for market. There were many large stumps in this field as well, but eventually, they were all removed. The soil, however, was rough, stony, uneven, and gravelly in certain areas, and once, when Michael Wilson brought over his Ford-Ferguson tractor to begin some plowing, the large rocks, boulders, and roots soon ended the operation.

The large clearing between the two cottages and the river produced fine crops of hay over the years; potatoes and fodder corn were also planted now and then, and upstream was a most productive vegetable patch, where raspberries, rhubarb, currants, and gooseberries grew. This garden was abandoned in 1929, when Mr. H.A. Ross and his wife, the former Jennie Butchart, bought that portion of the riverfront, and the guesthouse was built. Previously, a two-room cabin had been built that could be used by the Rosses during the summer months, but which could be used if necessary as an overflow for visitors at Greendale. Later, Mrs. Ross, (then a widow) had a water system installed, and a two-car garage built.

CHAPTER ONE

The Early Days

*(How the Greens came to live in the
frontier village of Lake Cowichan)*

Frank Green Arrives

*I*n referring to the early days at Greendale, I must include a full account of the history of my father's background.

His parents, two brothers and five sisters lived at Lisburn, in County Antrim, Ireland, and in the year 1885, he and a cousin, by the name of Bill Swinerton, left their homeland for the United States, landing at Portland, Maine. They travelled by train to San Francisco and with limited funds managed to buy a small two-wheeled cart and an old horse and travelled north along the Pacific coast, selling various odds and ends in the small villages through which they passed.

Upon reaching Seattle, Bill Swinerton continued on to Vancouver Island, but my father remained in Seattle for a time, working with a survey crew that was laying out new highways and streets around the city.

Later, he, too, reached Vancouver Island, where Victoria became his headquarters. Whilst there, he travelled north to Duncan, presumably by boat to Maple Bay since there was no road north from Goldstream, and managed to reach Cowichan Lake by a rough trail. He was impressed by what he saw, but felt that he wished to see more of the world before settling down. This involved a return to Seattle and a passage by sailing ship to Sydney, Australia, a voyage of six weeks.

There was no lack of jobs in Sydney, where the countryside was being developed in terms of highways and my father was impressed by the hospitality of the natives and the attractions of Sydney.

However, during his sojourn in Australia he learned that his parents, brothers, and sisters had left Ireland to take up residence in Victoria. He made the decision to join forces with them, and began the long and slow journey by sailing vessel back to Seattle and across to Victoria.

The intrepid Frank Green turned his back on the city and moved to the Cowichan Lake area and, once he got a taste of pioneering, he stayed there for the rest of his life.

His parents, meanwhile, had settled in a house on North Park Street, but his two brothers, Charles and Alfred, had been impressed by what my father had written concerning Cowichan Lake and the Cowichan Valley in general, and so had moved here to build the first Riverside Inn on the river. The present Riverside is the third one, the two previous having been destroyed by fire, but the location has never altered.

In the summer of 1887 my uncles persuaded one of

their sisters to come from Victoria in the role of cook, housekeeper, and hostess in which capacity she served admirably. There was no bridge across the river at that time but one fine summer day, she had a free afternoon, and decided to row across the river in the hotel boat and explore the magnificent forest of gigantic Douglas fir and cedar trees that extended in all directions. She was perhaps halfway across the stream and was looking for a suitable spot to land the boat when she saw three wolves on the shore, gazing at her intently. She returned to the haven of the hotel with all possible speed.

My father felt that he should join forces with his siblings, so for several years he operated a sort of stagecoach between Cowichan Lake and Duncan, making two trips per week and taking passengers, outgoing mail and light freight, whatever that might prove to be. It took four hours to reach Duncan and by far the greater part of the route was enclosed by the wonderful forest of native conifers.

Travelling between Lake Cowichan and Duncan in the early days involved a ride in Frank Green's Democrat wagon

He would spend the night in Duncan and make the return trip to the Lake the next morning, usually accompanied by passengers and the incoming mail bag. Deer and occasionally bears might be seen en route but the protective forest was also a shield in a sense when the snowfall was heavy.

Eventually he found himself driving Miss Louisa Spencer and her friend, Miss Frampton, through the majestic and glorious forest when they came north from Victoria, having been invited for a visit to Cowichan Lake. They finally arrived at Greendale, which at that time had not been named.

Years later, when I was exploring the forest across the highway to Duncan, I came upon a large cedar stump on which, skillfully carved, was the name "Erina", which I suppose was my father's first choice of a name for his land at Cowichan Lake.

Mother and her friend were enchanted by what they discovered during their short visit: the beautiful clear-flowing river, the stately forest on the opposite shore, the lofty mountains in the distance, the small island in mid-stream, to mention just a few of the more obvious attractions.

As the months passed, Frank Green and Louisa Spencer met frequently in Victoria, and found that they shared much in common. They were married in 1909 in Duncan.

My brother, Brian, was born in Victoria in 1910 and I in 1912. By this time some of the family property down the river near Little Beach had been sold and with the proceeds more land was cleared at Greendale and fruit trees planted, most of which are still living. Very slight depressions in the big lawn between the houses and the river indicate where huge stumps were laboriously burned out by the two Chinese labourers long ago, and now the remaining roots have rotted away, causing the soil to settle.

The beauty of Greendale is a delight to photographers and artists like Kathy Green, who painted this landscape of her grandmother's home.

The old barn has been converted over the decades to become a garage, a shed for Tony's boat, a store room for Yvonne's supply of preserved fruit, jelly, and jam. The lawnmowers and a large collections of garden tools are also kept there, and there is always extra room in the hayloft for various odds and ends. The barn was occupied by numerous cows, work horses, and by one or two goats, when goats' milk was considered to be very nutritious.

When brother Brian and I were attending school, Mother decided that a further source of income other than farm produce was becoming essential so two small cabins were built, each with two bedrooms and a porch facing south.

The first guests were fishermen, arriving in March, and staying for several weeks, returning for the fall run in September and early October. But during July and August the two cottages were used by families from Victoria and farther afield, bringing their children and other relatives. They all enjoyed the quiet, peaceful lifestyle and the proximity of the river.

In this way, as the guest books from the 1920s to the 1940s testify, Greendale became widely known as a fishing and holiday resort and we were able to share the beauty of the Cowichan Lake area with a wide variety of visitors.

Louisa makes her Way to the Lake

My mother, Louisa Spencer, was born in 1873, in St. Athan, Glamorganshire, Wales. Her parents, Michael and Fanny Spencer, owned a small farm there, but later moved across the Bristol Channel to Somerset, England, where they lived for some years at Monkton Manor Farm, in the village of Stogursey.

After the death of her father, the family moved to Taunton, and the children, one son and seven daughters, attended various schools to further their education. Louie, as she was known, attended a boarding school in Bradford, Yorkshire, where an uncle and several cousins had established themselves previously.

In those distant days, after graduation, there were few jobs or positions that a young girl might consider without risking social suicide; one might become successful as a governess, or a nurse, or a stenographer, but to work in a shop or as a waitress would indeed have been a step backwards. Louie was anxious to be independent, rather than to follow the sheltered and uneventful existence of her family in Taunton, and the restrictions of the 1890s. She was even much criticized by her mother and elder sisters for having bought a bicycle, and riding it in public.

Therefore, she became a governess to the young children of several prosperous families and this involved delightful interludes in the Scottish highlands, visits to London, and memorable holidays on the south and west coasts of England. She had studied music at school, and became an accomplished pianist, which was yet another qualification for a governess.

The most memorable interlude occurred when she accepted the post of an English-speaking governess to a wealthy Russian family living in Moscow. This was indeed a great adventure, and a rare experience for any young woman, for in those days to travel through Europe, un-chaperoned, was inviting danger or so her family were convinced.

Her employer was affiliated with the well-known firm of Fabergé, court jewelers to Czar Nicholas II, and his lifestyle was a most gracious one, with a fine town house, with many servants, and a comfortable abode in the country in which to spend the summers. But beneath this pleasant facade, there were symptoms of discontent, for even in comparative luxury, the servants had no bedrooms of their own, but slept in blankets on the floors of the kitchen regions. The Romanovs, particularly the Czarina, were hated by many, and political unrest and strife were sometimes evident.

After having lived for perhaps two years in Moscow, and having mastered the rudiments of the difficult language, it was with much regret that Louie returned to the family home in Taunton, due to her mother's failing health.

Previous to these incidents cousins from Victoria, B.C. had been travelling in England, and established acquaintance with members of the Spencer tribe. These were the sons of David Spencer, uncle to Louisa, who

Brave Louisa Spencer took a chance and traveled to Czarist Russia to act as a governess for an important family, learning the language and experiencing the pre-revolutionary culture of this eastern European power.

years before had founded the chain of Spencer's Stores in Victoria and Nanaimo, and on the Mainland.

Friendships had developed, and the Victoria family had issued warm invitations and offers of hospitality to those who might consider, in the future, a visit to Canada. After the death of her mother, the sale of the family home in Taunton, and a term as governess to a notable family in Shropshire, Louie felt the urge to travel again, this time to Canada, and more particularly to Victoria, where there was a promise of a post as governess to the two small children of Captain C.D. Neurotsos, in the service of the C.P.R.

Thus in 1906, she left from Liverpool for Montreal, sailing on the S.S. Virginia; among the passengers she met an Irishman, travelling similarly to Victoria, B.C., who spoke in glowing terms of the free and challenging life in the new outpost.

Upon arrival in the city, she found a warm welcome awaiting her with the Spencer cousins, then resident in what is now the Victoria Art Gallery on Moss Street. They were most kind and warm-hearted, and she found much of interest and delight in the New World, especially the freedom from hide-bound restrictions, and the opportunity to be individual.

The position of governess with the Neurotsos children continued for perhaps a year, until the young folk had outgrown the need for such guidance, and after that Louie decided to study to become a secretary. This involved mastering shorthand, and using a dictaphone, a new innovation in those days, and positions in offices in Vancouver and Tacoma followed, after which came a return to Victoria, where she became secretary to Justin Gilbert, the court reporter at that time.

During her first year in Victoria, she met, through the Irish travelling-companion, his cousins, a family named Green, similarly from Ireland and consisting of elderly parents, three sons, and five daughters. The eldest of the sons, Francis J. Green, (Frank) was at this time living at Cowichan Lake, where his two brothers had built the first Riverside Inn.

Eventually he and Louisa Spencer came to meet, at the Green home on North Park Street, in Victoria. His accounts of the pioneer life in the backwoods of Vancouver Island she found fascinating and challenging, and in due course, accompanied by one of her close friends as chaperone, she made her first visit to what was destined to be her future home. The journey was made by train to Duncan's— as it was then named—and then by horse and stage to the Lake.

Fresh from city life, visiting ladies are entranced by the beauty of the Cowichan Valley's deep woods.

Needless to say, the magnificent forest of virgin timber, the tranquil lake, and the beautiful river, more than exceeded the highest expectations of the emigree from England.

Both she and Frank Green shared the same longing for independence, freedom, and the challenge of the pioneer way of life, the benefits of which were not to be found in the city.

They were married in October, 1909, at St. Peter's Church, Quamichan, the sole attendees being the members of the Henry March family of Cowichan Lake. Life in those primitive days was not too easy; the business of clearing land, of burning out huge stumps, of patiently wresting a few more yards of ground for planting fruit trees, and crops, was exhausting and time consuming.

At the same time, Frank Green drove the horse-stage to Duncan. Since this routine included an overnight stop in Duncan, Louie Green would occasionally walk through the stately towering forest trail to what was known as "The Halfway Crossing", 10 miles distant, to meet her husband on his return to the Lake!

This was a totally different way of life for the young wife, raised in a sheltered atmosphere in England. The skills of cooking were unknown to her, the daily chores in the small log cabin must needs be dealt with, and later, the upbringing and caring for two small boys became another focus of her busy life, but she faced these challenges with faith and with courage, and seldom indulged in longing for her homeland.

There were few other women in the area then. Frank's brother and sister-in-law lived nearby, and a Colonel and Mrs. Haggard occupied a summer home downstream, but the pioneer Henry March family, her closest friends, lived all of eight miles distant, beyond Honeymoon Bay, so that contacts with these worthy folk were very infrequent.

As the years passed, it became evident that the pioneer life at Greendale, on the river, could never be prosperous, and with her two sons' futures to consider, Louie Green envisioned a plan of operating a sort of summer camp, or guesthouse, on the property. Proximity to the river and its excellent fishing areas, the wonderful lake, the abundance of game for the sports-minded, the peaceful surroundings and atmosphere all suggested that this venture might prove to be a success.

The word 'hotel' had a different meaning in Lake Cowichan's early days as can be seen by the Riverside Inn, left. However, these hunters are obviously enjoying their stay.

Although the two hotels, The Lakeside and the Riverside Inn were most popular, by 1890 there seemed room for yet another resort on the upper stretches of the river. (And also, before his marriage, Frank Green had catered to occasional transient fishermen and hunters, all of whom had appreciated his warm hospitality.)

Thus, in 1917, Louie Green began catering to her first visitors.

From then on, her life became more and more involved. Several guest cottages were built, tents were acquired for summer overflow, there were countless meals to prepare, and further housekeeping routines to be followed, until by mid-October, the last fisherman had departed. Then a hiatus of several months ensued, until, by early March, the season would commence again.

The passing years saw gradual improvements at Greendale; a telephone was installed, a bathroom with an adequate supply of hot and cold water became a necessity, in 1929 the first car made its appearance, and radio had invaded most of the homes in the area. Frank Green was less enthusiastic than his wife concerning the new venture, but he, too, was never idle.

There were several cows to care for, as well as chickens and horses, there was a large and most productive vegetable garden, and ever and always the urgent task of providing firewood for the main house, with its sturdy kitchen range and fireplace, as well as for the guest cottages.

From the early 1920s, as the business prospered, a cook was engaged to serve from mid-March until mid-September, by which time the Victoria families, with their many children, had returned to the city, and Louie could cope, single-handed, until the season closed in October.

Many warm friendships were established between the Greens and their guests over the years, friendships that have carried over into the next generations. Many were the fishermen who would appear over and over again, year after year, for those were the days when the Cowichan River was known worldwide, for the excellence of its trout-fishing.

A brief visit to England, in the winter of 1927, convinced Louie Green that without doubt, Vancouver Island had truly become home to her; it seemed as if English country life had become more than ever restricted and insular. The country itself was no less beautiful, but with husband and sons at Greendale, and many close friends, she was happy to return from the homeland to await the busy spring season of 1928.

Thus the years passed, and gradual changes were evident in the community. The two railway lines cancelled their passenger service since an improved highway and bus system became too competitive, and also by then most residents owned their own cars. Hydro power in the village, with its many labor-saving gadgets, was a decided step forward. In addition, families were less inclined to spend several weeks in one spot during the holiday season; the new car and the lure of the highway enabled them to cover far more territory.

In 1947, Frank Green died at the age of 86. For some years thereafter Louie continued to live at Greendale, where occasional visitors appeared, usually in the fishing-season. By way of a diversion, she resumed teaching piano pupils, and looked forward to the weekly visits of the young students. In 1963, she moved to a rest home at Cherry Point, south of Duncan, where she passed away in January 1965, at the age of 92.

This old family portrait shows many of the earliest Greens.

A Fascinating Cast of Characters

*W*hose decision was it, I wonder, that caused them all to assemble, on that fine long-ago morning, beneath the huge oak tree at Victoria's Beacon Hill Park? Perhaps they did not have far to go, for they must have been still living on Heywood Avenue then, and the cricket pitch, and its broad expanse of sloping meadow and distant shrubbery lay just across the street. They had taken with them four chairs, and a fur rug for those in the front row to recline upon. It must, I think, have been spring, for the limbs of the great oaks are leafless, and they are too lightly dressed for a cold winter's morning. Skene-Lowe, *the* photographer of that distant era, had posed them formally, the patriarch and two of his sons standing in the back row; the old mother, her daughter and son, and young grandson (Rollie) occupying the chairs, and in the front row, Lawrence Gulline, and the three sisters, Nellie, Nan, and Kitty. There they are: the Green family of Lisburn, County Antrim, Ireland, perhaps ten years after they had settled in Victoria.

Standing at the left of the back row is Uncle Charlie, gazing far off at something distant; he wears a dark bowler hat, a long black frock coat, slightly wrinkled at the sleeves, a white shirt, and wide white cravat. I never saw him. He was reputed to be a "lady-killer", with an immense fund of charm that few could resist. He worked hard and with great dedication in establishing the pioneer Riverside Inn at Cowichan Lake, and some years later, when sight and health were failing, had made a trip to Seattle to hear an inspiring address by the noted theologian and mystic, Mrs. Annie Besant. Some days later, returning to Victoria from Port Townsend, he was drowned with many others, when the small steamer Clallam encountered a terrific storm south of Trial Island, and foundered during a night of horror and panic.

Next to him stands my grandfather, a fine-looking and hearty old man.

So far as I know, we did not ever meet, although he was no stranger to the Cowichan Valley, living for a short time at the old Forrest farm near Hillbank. Did he leave the Emerald Isle in doubt and trepidation of the future that lay ahead, or was he anxious to make his mark as a prosperous citizen of the New World? This we can never know, but it would seem, over the succeeding generations, that none of the Greens were destined to be "rich", perhaps because none would have chosen to be. With few notable exceptions, they chose, instead, humility and simplicity; they would not have known what to do with wealth.

Next to my grandfather stands the man with whom, of all the family, I was best acquainted, my father, Francis Jacob Green. In order to appear on the same level as his father and brother, he must have been standing on a tussock of grass, or perhaps a root of the gnarled oak, for he was of small stature. He, too, is dressed, in the prevailing style, a rakish bowler hat, a long dark topcoat, and wide cravat. In the several decades we shared together, I seldom, if ever, saw him formally attired. His life was wholly blended with the hardy, pioneer existence at Cowichan, where the dictates of custom and fashion were, to him, meaningless and trivial.

Below these three, in the next row, sprawled on a chair in an indolent attitude, sits Alfred Abram Green, (Uncle Alf). His hands, one of which clasps a pipe, are crossed over his elegant cane; I can detect a ring on one finger, and he seems to have gloves, or a handkerchief, with which to cushion the top of the cane. His suit is of some dark cloth, with a high-fitting collar, and a wide, loosely knotted tie, a forerunner of the fashionable but smaller bow ties of the Terrible Twenties. He, of the assembled males, (apart from young Rollie) is the only one wearing a cap. Uncle Alf is gazing intently in front of him, the ends of his dark, luxuriant moustache appear to be waxed. He was, I believe, the tallest of the family, well over six feet. Was he, at this time, I wonder, courting his future wife, the vivacious and handsome Dorothy Berridge (later to be known as "Aunt Doll")? They were married, I think, a few years before my parents, and lived in a comfortable log cabin, high above the Cowichan River. They had no children, but their close friends suggested that a child could have added no further happiness to their life together.

But that was long ago, and years later, I can just recall the day when Uncle Alf, in his Army uniform, called in to say goodbye before leaving for duty overseas. By then, he and Aunt Doll were drifting further and further apart, and thus the enforced separation seemed to be the only possible solution. He was killed by a sniper's bullet in 1916, I think, and lies buried somewhere in France. Aunt Doll received the news with admirable and characteristic composure; she was in Victoria at the time, about to keep an appointment with the dentist, when the message came by telephone from the war office. She turned to her sister, and said, "Alf's gone," and then, after a moment, "Well, we'd better go, can't keep the dentist waiting" and it was as if, from then on, Alf had never existed. She lived on for years at the log cabin on the hill; she lived as she pleased, she did as she wished. She was strong, self-willed, a man's woman, and the malicious and idle gossip directed at her from time to time, was powerless to influence her in any way. Although my father, and Aunts Nan, Kitty, and Pollie treated her with their habitual, well-bred politeness and deference, this was simply because she had been Alf's wife; they didn't, I think, really like her. (But my brother, Brian, and I, too young to be aware of anything about Aunt Doll that might be considered questionable, liked her very much; we often paid her Saturday morning visits, assured of a welcome, and the added dividend of cookies, or a slab of chocolate cake.)

Beside Alf, sitting aloof and perhaps a trifle withdrawn, is Aunt Sallie. Years later, after her death, people still spoke of her legendary beauty and charm, her grace and dignity. She, of the assembled company, is by far the best dressed; a smart hat crowning her luxuriant hair, a fur collar to her coat, and a fur muff. But she is gazing off to the right, oblivious to the camera. What had attracted her attention? Was she thinking of Willy Whyte, and her broken marriage, or was this before his sudden departure? Willy Whyte was what would now be termed "a smooth operator". He worked in the offices of the formidable Robert Dunsmuir, who had by then amassed a fortune from the coal mines at Nanaimo and the connecting railway line. Willy Whyte and Aunt Sallie lived in a fine house on Richardson Street, not so many blocks from the resplendent Dunsmuir Castle, (Craigdarroch Castle) which must have been then a-building. Was he then, I wonder, plotting and planning the nefarious stratagems that culminated in his hasty flight from Victoria, with a few thousand Dunsmuir dollars, concealed upon his person, in addition to Aunt Sallie's jewelry, and leaving a mountain of debt behind? It was believed that he had found refuge in South America, (under an assumed name) but in all events, he was never heard of again.

Grandmother Sarah Green.

And so Aunt Sallie and her little boy, Rollie, were obliged to leave the Richardson Street house, and begin a new life. In time, she managed to secure a secretarial job in an office in town, and after a few years married her employer, a highly respected man named Duncan Irving. But their happiness was short lived, for Aunt Sallie was stricken by a terminal illness, leaving a wide circle of relatives and friends to mourn her passing.

Standing next to her is Rollie Whyte, her son, a tow-haired lad of perhaps eight or nine, wearing a modified version of a sailor suit, and a dark, tight fitting cap. Rollie, like so many of the Green family, was highly thought of and respected; his father's rejection in no way warped his outlook on life. For many years, his modest home in Foul Bay was a haven for countless friends. His life as a surveyor took him into many remote sections of the mainland and of Vancouver Island. Again, he was not rich in what are termed this world's goods, but his charm and genuine consideration for others *were* priceless qualities. He had great respect, admiration and affection for my father, who was very good to his young nephew, bringing him up the long, winding road through the forest in the ancient rig from Duncan to spend happy summer weeks at Cowichan. During my father's last illness, Rollie was a tower of strength and understanding, visiting him countless times at St. Joseph's Hospital, and later at Duncan. And now Rollie is gone, but his fine qualities are perpetuated in his children, and, I am sure, in his grandchildren.

Next to Rollie, on the right, sits my grandmother, Sarah Remington Green, her husband's hand resting protectively on her shoulder. She appears to be wearing a voluminous dark cloak and a Fez-shaped lace cap. The face is kind, mild and gentle, unseamed by the lines and scars of ambition and worldliness. I remember her vaguely as a very old and frail woman, a pallid and transparent ghost, with the hot and trembling hands of the aged. She had long been widowed by then, and lived with her daughter, Kitty, and son-in-law, Douglas Muir, on Robertson Street, in Foul Bay. Again, I wonder if she was happy and adjusted to life in the New World, or whether heart and soul and thoughts were in Ireland?

Next to grandmother, likewise perched on a parlor chair, is Caroline Remington Green, the youngest of the family, known as "Wee Kitty". Dear Aunt Kitty: her gaiety, her charm, her kindness are cherished memories over many years. Here, Kitty looks perhaps 17 or 18; she is faintly smiling, an embarrassed little smile. She wears a black dress, with full, heavy skirt, a white blouse with enormous leg-of-mutton sleeves, a tight black choker collar, and a large cameo brooch. Her hat, like that of her sister Sallie, is perched on her head, a strange and wonderful creation in black and white. She is holding her gloves in one hand, so that the day could not have been too cold. Dear Aunt Kitty: the happy Saturday mornings spent at her hospitable home on Robertson Street, where lemonade, cake and cookies were lavishly offered, remain with me as sunny interludes during my high school years in Victoria. Her passing, as unexpected as it was untimely, was a source of great grief and sorrow to her devoted family. Aunt Kitty possessed, in full measure, those innate characteristics of the Green women: charm, dignity, poise and grace, tempered with humor and humility, a perfect blending into a special sort of quality. (I can think of no other words.)

Now, we reach the front row of the family group, and here we have Uncle Lawrence Gulline, his wife, Aunt Nellie, and finally Aunt Nan, who, next to my father, I knew best of all. Uncle Lawrence, who appears something of a dandy, with his black bowler hat, and polished Malacca cane, is sprawled out on the somewhat tattered-looking fur hearthrug, brought, no doubt, from before the fireplace in the Heywood Avenue house for the occasion. I have no recollection of having ever met Uncle Lawrence nor Aunt Nellie, who had removed themselves to Montreal, long before I was born. Uncle Lawrence, so far as I know, in company with his two sons, Brian and Fryer, owned a sporting goods shop, and made a specialty of dealing in fishing-rods, and hand-tied fishing flies.

Aunt Nellie, here seated beside Lawrence, is enveloped in a heavy tweedy-looking coat, with great bell sleeves and wide revers; her hat is a tiny affair, barely visible at the back of her head, and seems to be made from a polka-dot material. All I know for certain about Aunt Nellie is that a pair of gumboots, sacrosanct gumboots I should add, which once belonged to her, were stored away in a cupboard, not to be touched.

Long after her death, the gumboots lingered on, as if they must be held in readiness, lest their owner return to claim them. But the strong family ties that have bound the Greens together for many years and several generations, have proven oblivious to time and distance, for though Montreal and the Cowichan Valley are a vast distance apart, nevertheless, we at Cowichan were privileged to meet two of Aunt Nellie's three children; Cousin Fryer, shortly before World War Two, and his elder sister, Eileen (Kenney), three years ago. Fryer was then perhaps in his late twenties or early thirties and possessed in abundance the charm, the humor, and the warmth of his forebears. It was his first visit to British Columbia and the Island, and he was loud in his enthusiasm of all that he saw and did. He and my father got along famously together; they, in company with Rollie Whyte seemed to speak a special language of their own, the sort of language in which the fluency of words is unnecessary. We took Fryer for several long drives about the area;

he enjoyed the trout fishing in the river, and all in all, his visit was a great success. We saw him again, a few years later, during the war, when he was stationed for a short time at Nanaimo. He stayed with us for a weekend, I remember, and brought with him another young soldier. Again, he enjoyed the brief respite from the army barracks and a change of scene. But it was a vastly different situation from the happy visit of former years.

The whole world was in conflict and turmoil; one's thoughts and actions were colored by the war, and the outcome thereof. We, in our quiet backwater at Cowichan, were least affected, but for Fryer and his generation, the everyday world had crumbled. Beneath his gallant effort to be humorous and cheerful, he was tense and embittered, and unsure of himself, and unsure of his future. He felt that the months and years spent in the army were futile and wasted, and for him I am sure that they were. When he left, to be driven back to Nanaimo, we felt, perhaps, that we were seeing him for the last time. And so it proved, for a year or so later, he was swept away in some particularly lethal action in France, I believe, following in the footsteps of Uncle Alf, who fell at Vimy Ridge, perhaps 25 years before. "They gave their happy youth away, for Country and for God". There are those who can believe implicitly in these words, but there are thousands for whom the eternal question, "Why?" goes unanswered.

Years later, here at Greendale, we were privileged to meet his sister, Eileen Kenney, her husband, Theo, and sister-in-law, Dorothy, (the widow of Brian Gulline, whom we had never met.) They arrived at Greendale on a wet afternoon in May or early June. At once I became aware of Eileen's warmth and charm, her lively intelligence, her quick humor. At this time, she must have been approaching 70, but this was impossible to believe. I was fascinated by her memories of Greendale as she knew it, when, as a small girl, she came with her mother to stay with Uncle Frank. She remembered sleeping in a bunk bed in the old log sitting-room, and seeing the flickering flames from the log fire; she remembered the deer invading the vegetable garden every night; she remembered my father warning her and her mother on no account to go near the river alone because of the danger of cougar. With these and other anecdotes, the afternoon passed away all too soon. But the bond of warm friendship was firmly established, and what has been sometimes referred to as the clannishness of the Greens was further extended.

And last, but far from least, to the right foreground, seated on the hearthrug, is Annie Evelyn Green, "Aunt Nan", and it is with many mixed feelings that I write of her. Aunt Nan is gazing across the group towards some object on the left, beyond the range of the camera. What is it that she sees, or has the photographer requested her to look out left front? She looks curiously tranquil and relaxed; contented almost, as I never remember her during the three years that I boarded with her during my high school days in Victoria. But that episode was many years later, in the late 1920s, whereas the family group must have gathered under the big oak at Beacon Hill in or about 1887. Paragraphs, pages, and chapters could, and should, be written about Aunt Nan, for, though small and slight, she was wiry and dauntless in spirit, fiercely devoted to her immediate family. When aroused to anger, she could give as good as she got or even better.

My father often told us of how, in the old days in Antrim, Aunt Nan was the tomboy of the family, and raced and romped about the fields and hedge rows with her brothers. This spirit of rebellion or non-conformity guided Aunt Nan to Cowichan in 1885, where she proved to be a popular and capable hostess at the newly built Riverside Inn, thoroughly and passionately loving the adventurous pioneer way of life in the great forests of the Cowichan Valley. But when I first remember staying at Aunt Nan's, she and Aunt Pollie were living in a gloomy, gaunt, and aging house, bristling with bay windows and scrollwork, on Fernwood Road. Here she had planned to make a fair living by renting rooms, and providing board for high school and college students, but this brave effort was doomed to failure. True, the location was favorable, equidistant from Craigdarroch Castle, and the Fernwood High School, but the gloomy, austere atmosphere of the brooding, old house, and its dim, high-ceilinged rooms, repelled rather than attracted students, even in the far-off primitive era of the 1920s.

And so, at length, the aunts moved away from 1504 Fernwood Road, to another old house, again embellished with bay windows, jalousie blinds and scrollwork, on upper Fort Street. Here, my brother and I lodged with Aunt Nan and Aunt Pollie, while I attended Victoria High School, and he began his lengthy career with Ames & Co. But again, as I have said, several chapters are needed to provide a true portrait of Aunt Nan. It is sufficient to say, however, that there were many, many instances when she and I refused to see eye to eye, and our respective tempers and self-control were sorely tried. Her sense of duty, and her devotion and loyalty to her own kith and kin were dominant and grasping; she could not love, nor express affection without possessing. But she was hard working and self-sacrificing to a degree, and no drudgery nor humiliation was too great to be endured, if it might add to the happiness, or wellbeing of any member of her family.

In the family group, she looks serene, yet confident. It was well that she could not see far ahead to her later years, years of hardship, poverty and drudgery. Her fierce spirit of independence and determination carried her along, but sadness and loneliness, those inexorable companions of old age, came ever closer. And she lived to see them all go, her four sisters, her three brothers, and I think that a little of her died as each departed. The final years, lived out at the Aged Ladies' Home, at least provided the physical comforts: warmth, good meals, and a comfortable room. And I am certain that her memories, and "the bliss of solitude" helped the long days to pass more quickly.

I have not, as yet, mentioned Hannah Mary Green, (Aunt Pollie) because she was absent from home when the family assembled for the photograph. She had gone to Langley to stay with an elderly cousin, William Mackie, and his wife. Aunt Pollie was gay and beautiful, and possessed in ample measure, the particular charm and graciousness of the Greens. Yet her life, too, was to be touched by tragedy. From several eligible young bachelors of that era, she chose to become engaged to one Hal Berridge (a brother to Aunt Doll.) They had leased a house into which they were to move, following their wedding. One evening they had walked across to inspect the house, and found it locked.

Aunt Pollie, not to be thwarted, and assisted by Hal, contrived to push open a downstairs window. Somehow, in clambering up, or wrestling with the window, she fell, not far, but far enough, and in such a way to cause permanent spinal damage. She was in hospital for a lengthy interval, then finally returned home to embark on the life of a chronic invalid, and for the rest of her life, many hours of every day were spent in bed, or else lying on her bed, propped up with pillows. She was waited on and nursed devotedly by Aunt Nan, and gradually built up her own life, in which the world, and the things of the world ceased to exist. (In all fairness to Hal Berridge, it was Aunt Pollie who insisted on breaking off the marriage, for she refused to believe that any man could, or should, sacrifice his life to a helpless invalid. It sounds too sentimental to add that Hal Berridge died a drunkard, as I have heard, but it may be so!)

And so Aunt Pollie, as I came to know her, lay for hours and days on her bed, sometimes reading, sometimes knitting, or making dolls or stuffed animals for Rollie's children or for bazaars, occasionally going for short walks up and down Fort Street hill when the weather was fine. There were days when she suffered cruelly from sciatica, when no one but Aunt Nan might see her, but mostly I remember her, tranquil and serene, sitting upright on her bed, gracious and charming, and at times radiant. Her clothes were of a bygone era: high black laced boots for outdoor wear, long black skirts, an outmoded hat, and yet, despite this faded elegance, there was about her an air of quality and distinction that could not be denied. Eventually, she and Aunt Nan together found a final refuge at the Aged Ladies' Home on McClure Street, and perhaps these last years were not too desolate. And mercifully, the cancer that took her away at last was swift.

This, then, is a summary of the Green Family, who long ago assembled beneath the great oak tree at Beacon Hill Park. And now, we, the grandchildren of the two "Old People" from County Antrim, are getting along, as they say, approaching our sixties and seventies. How rapidly the stream of life flows past us, with its joys and sorrows, its ecstasies and tragedies. Customs and costumes change, our way of life changes; families, large or small, no longer gather under oak trees in city parks, with chairs and fur rugs, for a group picture. We are living in a far more challenging age, a frenetic age. To my grandchildren, this faded photograph will be ludicrous, an oddity, a museum piece; they will be embarrassed to think that these strange people, with their queer clothes and fixed expressions could possibly be their forbears.

If a summing-up be necessary, I can think of nothing more fitting than this couplet from Scott's "Lady of the Lake":

"Time rolls his ceaseless course. The race of yore,
Who danced our infancy upon their knee
And told our marveling boyhood legends store,
Of their strange ventures happed by land or sea,
How are they blotted from the things that be!
How few, all weak and withered of their force,
Wait, on the verge of dark eternity,
Like stranded wrecks, the tide returning hoarse
To sweep them from our sight!
Time rolls his ceaseless course."

CHAPTER TWO

Life on the River's Edge

Hewers of Wood

One morning, several years ago, when Hildegard Wood came over from the Old House to tell me that it was no longer possible to have a load of firewood delivered from any source nearer than Victoria, I simply could not believe my ears. What nonsense was this? How could it be? Here I had lived in the Cowichan Lake area, man and boy, for close to 60 years, and never in all that time had such a situation arisen. There had always been firewood available, and there always would be, or so I had believed, for was not the Cowichan Valley known afar as the Land of the Big Trees, and were there not three prosperous sawmills spewing out mill wood and sawdust and chips month after month, and year after year?

True, we had noticed that local deliveries of wood and sawdust seemed to have become less regular in recent months, but surely the supply could never totally cease. But Hildegard's report, as it turned out, was all too true. The Hillcrest Mill at Mesachie Lake had given up selling mill wood in any case, and now, it seemed, both the Youbou and the Honeymoon Bay mills would follow suit. And as for sawdust, there might be a limited supply from time to time, available from Youbou, and that would be mixed fir and cedar. Hemlock sawdust was more plentiful, but any fool knew how hopeless it was to use hemlock sawdust as fuel. It smoked, it refused to feed into the burner, and it produced but little heat. The best that Norman Wood had been able to do was to elicit a vague promise from an East Indian fuel merchant in Duncan that since even the huge sawmill at Chemainus no longer produced mill wood of any sort, he would try to bring us two loads of reasonably good fuel from Victoria!

Frank Green loved the frontier life of Greendale on the Cowichan River and was not always in a hurry to try new ideas but quickly grasped their utility once he saw them in use.

All this was shattering news indeed; we could not believe that firewood could be in such short supply, but in the end, we could only submit, and eventually a dilapidated old truck turned in at our driveway with our supply of winter fuel. It was not especially good wood, either, and certainly it was expensive. My father, I know, would have considered most of it to be very poor quality, and would have scorned to burn it in the ancestral fireplace at the old house. But we managed, nevertheless, and I am glad to report that no such acute situation has since arisen.

All this turmoil, however, made a great impression on me, and over and over again, I have thought back to my childhood and my early youth, when "rustling firewood" was simply part of the yearly routine.

My father firmly believed that any man, be he bachelor, or husband, or father, who was unable to provide his own firewood was worth his salt, as they used to say. And any pioneer who could not swing an axe nor file a saw had no business to be pioneering at all, and had better return to his town background forthwith. And certainly, my father lived up to these standards most nobly, and many months, if not years, of his life were spent at the laborious task of providing his family with firewood.

In retrospect, I can see now the importance of this endeavour, and the necessity of having a plentiful supply of wood stored away. For not only was there the kitchen range to feed, but the dining-room heater, and the large fireplace in the sitting room, as well as the small airtight heaters in the two guest cottages. And not only were there several wood boxes to be kept filled, but also the heavy work of bringing the freshly cut bush wood in from the forest. As the years passed, it was necessary to go farther afield for wood, eventually across the highway, and through the "near forest", across the railway tracks, and along the winding wood road up to the Big Trees.

These giant Douglas firs had been scorched years before in a great forest fire that had swept up the low range of mountains from Duncan, but few had been totally burned, and made the best of all possible fuel. In later years, I learned from my father the "pioneer" technique of felling one of these giants single-handed. Not always might the early pioneer depend on a working partner to share the labor of establishing the undercut, and later, finishing the project with the back cut. It is possible, I believe, for those of great stamina to operate the crosscut saw single-handed, but the free end must be braced against the axe handle, the axe having been driven deeply into the bark across from the faller, so that the saw will not sag. But it is slow and heavy work, and my father's system, albeit slower still, was less arduous.

In the early days, the forest surrounded Greendale but as the years passed, the Greens were able to clear more and more land.

Several times I watched him at work, and in later years, I have successfully burned out a number of old fir stumps that had been standing for years in the fields at home. First, father would study the tree carefully, to determine in which direction it was to fall (usually to the south, it seems to me). Then he would carefully chop out a section of the thick fire-scarred bark perhaps two feet above the ground level and clear away any tangled second-growth or salal brush. The next step took time and patience, for a hole, at least six inches deep, must be bored into the trunk with a two-inch auger, previously sharpened so that it would bite readily into the firm wood. As the auger penetrated the trunk, a delightful scent of fresh pitch resulted, and large chips emerged from the deepening hole which now and again must be cleared of shreds and fibres with a bent wire.

When the aperture was deep enough, a second hole was bored, perhaps a foot above the first, but angling sharply down, in order that the two holes would finally meet. All this procedure took some time, but at last, with a dramatic cracking sound, the auger broke through the thin partition of wood, into the far end of the first hole, and the job was completed. The next phase was to shave long slivers from a slab of pitchwood, ignite them, and feed them carefully into the lower hole, with the opening above acting as a chimney. Sometimes much puffing and blowing might be necessary to produce a good heat, and larger pitch slivers and sometimes dry cedar or shreds of fir bark were used as extra fuel. Eventually, however, the fire was established, and needed no further attention. A spiral of smoke issued from the little chimney, and encouraging muffled cracklings might be heard from within, and my father could return to the farm chores secure in the knowledge that the fire god was in total command of the situation.

Sometimes the tree would burn for several days, depending upon the quantity and the condition of the pitch (or resin) within its fibres. Before long, the two holes had joined together, and a fierce heat emanated, as from a small fireplace. And day by day, the cavity became larger and larger, the flames licking eagerly into the heartwood, until, as the hours passed, the gigantic trunk, no longer safely buttressed from below, began to lean from the perpendicular, to finally fall with a resounding crash, and a shattering of mighty limbs. Once or twice, I recall, the tree fell during the night, or in the early hours of the morning, but at that time there need be no concern for adjacent property. The wood-lot was far away from our nearest neighbour.

Once the forest giant had fallen, usually the fire extinguished itself, and the next phase was to limb the branches, many of which would have provided us with many ricks of fine fuel. And then for my father came the laborious work of cutting the great tree, block by block, with his faithful crosscut saw.

Often he would take a sandwich lunch with him, light a fire to brew his noonday cup of tea, and be away until mid-afternoon, with his faithful collie dog for company. On wet days he worked beneath a flimsy roof of sheet-iron, which must needs be moved as each fresh cut was started. Then, of course, each block must be split with axe, long-handled sledgehammer, and steel wedge, and the slabs loaded into the old horse-drawn farm wagon, to finally be thrown into the woodshed at home. Nor was that the end, for each slab of wood must be chopped into smaller sizes to fit into the firebox of the kitchen range, or the various heaters. Then there was kindling to be split as well, and there were ashes to be removed from time to time, and stovepipes and chimneys to be cleaned. Indeed and truly, the hewers of wood had little time for idleness.

But during the early 1920s, this primitive method and its attendant hard labor inevitably yielded to the march of progress, which came about in this way.

One afternoon, my parents' busy daily routine was interrupted by the arrival of a visitor, from Duncan, one Charles Bazett, who had known my father for some years, although their paths did not cross often. Conversation and reminiscence flowed easily, however, and Mr. Bazett readily accepted an invitation to spend the night, appearing more than willing to assist with the farm chores. And for the next several years he was a frequent visitor, when pressures of his auctioneering business occasionally relaxed, and he was able to seek refuge from what we gathered was domestic infelicity strained to the breaking point. Mrs. Bazett, we gathered, was *difficile* in the extreme and, at times, the two grown daughters and son could be additional thorns in the flesh.

But for Mr. Bazett, the way of escape lay through his involvement with religion. I must explain that at this time, there flourished in the United States a faith or cult known as Unity, (not to be confused with the Unitarians). The mother church, or the fountainhead, was the Unity School of Christianity, located in

Tracy, Mo., and flourishing branches were established throughout the West, as well as across Canada. The Victoria stronghold was entrenched on an upper floor of the Campbell Building, where a saintly old lady, by the name of Mrs. Gordon Grant, reigned supreme. And of the satellites and disciples, none was more dedicated than Mr. Bazett. In time, he prevailed upon my parents to at least, subscribe to monthly periodicals, in which important features were the "healing thought", and the "prosperity thought", and many another worthy precept. There was, I am sure, much to be said in praise of Unity, and, as has been said of other newborn faiths, "at least, it can do no harm," and I am sure that Mr. Bazett was much sustained thereby through times of stress.

But as time passed, brother Brian and I became skeptical. If Mr. Bazett held the prosperity thought devoutly, why did he continue to drive a shabby, rattling old Model "T" Ford, and why did he wear garments of rusty black that reeked of mothballs, and a sleazy string tie? We had, I fear, reached that stage of development that caused us to judge people by their possessions and not by their characters. If Mr. Bazett had appeared one day driving a brand-new Hudson or a Buick, we would have been most favorably and suitably impressed. True, we did derive a sadistic joy in seeing Mr. Bazett struggling to crank the stubborn Model "T" one wet morning, until finally, the coil was removed from a mysterious black box beneath the dashboard, and brought indoors to dry in the warming oven.

To be honest, brother Brian and I did not really care for Mr. Bazett. We thought his occasional offerings of a nickel, or more rarely, a dime, were unimpressive in the extreme. To us, he seemed fussy, nervous, and boring, especially when we were obliged to listen to his ministrations to some "poor little woman", who had appealed to him for help due to some adverse circumstances or through bereavement. At such times, Brian's term for the good man was "kittenish" and I think that we both felt some trace of sympathy for the much maligned Mrs. Bazett.

But this aside, there was the bond of mutual friends to be considered, and certainly the neighbours of whom Mr. B. spoke formed a socially impeccable group: the Stokers, the Leathers, the Kingstons, the Whittomes, and the Jayneses. He knew them all, and frequently referred to them.

Another reason why my brother and I were not drawn to Mr. Bazett was more obscure, yet one that could not be wholly overlooked. For the unfortunate man was completely ignorant, I am sure, of a grievous social affliction, which in refined society was never mentioned. In this frank age, the condition would have been summarily dismissed in just two simple words: a breath problem, but long ago, modesty forbade such honesty. Instead, it was only discreet advertisements for Listerine Mouthwash and Lavoris, appearing in more refined magazines, that offered helpful suggestions such as "Always a bridesmaid, but never a bride?", "He turned his head away", and "If you want the truth, go to a child". These admonitions, along with shadowy illustrations of the afflicted, no doubt helped to boost the sale of the product in question, but for Mr. Bazett there seemed no redemption. Delicately nurtured ladies, in conversation with the sprightly gentleman, were seen to raise their eyes piously to Heaven and permit themselves a faint and patient smile.

But perhaps I am being unkind and unjust in my evaluation of Mr. Bazett, for basically, he was a kindly man, and, I am sure, he earnestly tried to "so let his Light shine before Men". Therefore, perhaps a year or so after his first visit, he persuaded my parents to seriously consider investing in a drag saw, not only as a labour-saving device, but as a genuine investment, producing many dividends in time saved, and vast supplies of firewood with far less effort. This all took much persuasion, however. My father was perfectly satisfied with the Old Ways, my mother reluctant to deplete the family coffers by the $300, a fortune in those days, with which to pay for the drag saw. But Mr. Bazett's persuasions, urged on, no doubt, by the prosperity thought, won out, and at last arrived the Great Day, when my father returned from the railway station, the drag saw in its crate, on the floor of the wagon.

I think that Brian and I were slightly disappointed to learn that our new acquisition was not a majestic Wee McGregor, a proud name in the roster of drag saws, but rather, a lesser version, named "Li'l Husky", a product of the Vaughan Motor Works, Vancouver. The Dunsmuirs and the Marches possessed Wee McGregors, as did by then most of the logging camps in the Valley, but the Greens, it seemed, were destined to go through life with a Li'l Husky, the poor relation of the drag saw hierarchy.

Yet when the Li'l Husky was assembled, before the trial run, it was not without a certain flair. The wood frame was painted a cheerful shade of red, the one-cylinder motor, mounted amidships, a vivid green. And there were embellishments of highly polished brass: the oiler, for example, located over the cylinder, the throttle control, the governor and the clutch lever: each of these gleamed like the rising sun. Then there were the several grease cups, adjacent to certain vital bearings. The batteries, a foursome of dry cells, were tucked away in a compartment ahead of the motor, next to the coil, in its highly varnished wooden case. And the gasoline and water tanks were brightly painted containers, side by side, above the battery box and the two steel dogs, which were driven firmly into the log to hold the machine firmly, and to lessen vibration.

I know that my father did not take kindly to the Internal Combustion Engine in general. He had a deep-seated respect for the explosive and incendiary qualities of gasoline in any form, and he had always kept a discreet distance from cars and trucks, be they old or new. Sooner or later, he was convinced, they would catch on fire, or else they would explode, and thus he wished no part of them. Therefore, it was all the more to his credit that grudgingly, and with some trepidation, he mastered the challenge of the Li'l Husky. Our next-door neighbor (Jack Hatter) who, when necessary, operated the Dunsmuir Wee McGregor, was generous with his knowledge and advice to augment the basic principles outlined in the instruction booklet.

And so, one memorable autumn afternoon as I walked home from school, I heard as I approached our property, the unmistakable sound of an internal combustion engine in operation. I hurried along the trail through the woods and arrived in time to join a little group: my parents, Jack Hatter, and Mr. Bazett, who had presented himself for the occasion, the "auspicious occasion", I should have said. The Li'l Husky was sprawled obscenely upon a prostrate log that had been lying for several years on the damp ground. Steam from the water jacket funneled forth, combined with the strong smell of exhaust, and the heavy saw-blade swept back and forth, slicing through the log with abandon. Certainly, no more effective demonstration could have been planned for in a matter of an hour, the drag saw had accomplished what would have taken my father several days to do. How, then, could he be other than greatly impressed?

Thus, the drag saw became a valued ally in the work program, and over the years, I came to know and to understand it well. Seldom did it falter, and only once, I think, did it require a major overhaul. Its limitations seemed to be few. Yes, certainly, it was cumbersome and despite the company's proud boast that it was a One-Man Saw, I am sure that Charles Atlas in his prime would have struggled in vain to hoist it into the wagon, or to drag it through the underbrush to a new field of operation. My father filed the blade from time to time and, when not in use, the machine was protected from the elements by a cover or shelter made of corrugated iron and two burlap sacks. Memories of my youth include brilliant summer mornings, trundling up to the woodlot, with the creaking old wagon, drawn by Sandy, the slow-moving old horse, to haul home the newly split wood, in its layer of fire-scarred bark. How seldom one sees firewood such as this today.

Even today, Lake Cowichan is surrounded by forests but in the early part of the 20th century, the trees were older and darker, crowding the small village.

When, some years later, I was working in the village, there was no time for the hewing of wood, mechanically or otherwise. It was too much for my father to handle alone, and Sandy, ancient of days, had vanished from the scene. And by this time there were one or two wood merchants in the village, who delivered wood to one's very door, a great convenience for the working family. For a short time, we experimented with burning oil in the kitchen range but with little success. It was expensive, it was slow to heat, and so the next transition was to sawdust as a fuel, which involved further conversion of the old range. For several years, sawdust proved to be the ideal fuel: inexpensive and unfailing in supply, offering controlled heat, and instant response to the adjusting of air-drafts.

Before many more years had passed, however, sawdust became impossible to buy, and the wood merchants slowly faded from the scene. More and more homes were heated electrically, or by oil-fired furnace, and I well remember my poor daughter's humiliation, when she was obliged to confess to her sophisticated classmates that her parents, who dwelt in a funny old house on Greendale Road, *still* burned wood in their kitchen stove, and what was even more embarrassing, they scrounged their supplies of firewood themselves!

But again, the truth of the old saying, "The more things change, the more they remain the same" is revealed; and now, in the 1980s, in part due to the widespread evils of inflation, more and yet more people are returning to wood, in various forms, for their heating and cooking requirements. Not a day passes but one may see several trucks or small pickups speeding through our village laden with freshly split wood, or newly cut blocks. It is fashionable to enclose one's fireplace with a Fisher or a Jötul wood burner, or one of a dozen other makes, guaranteed to provide sustaining heat with a minimum of attention. The crosscut saw, the Wee McGregor and the Li'l Husky are museum pieces today, and the efficient portable chainsaw reigns supreme. Such makes as Stihl, Husqvarna, Homelite, Pioneer, and McCulloch strive for dominance in the sales market; each has its good points and its limitations.

And so the circle has come full once more, and we are back to the hewing of wood in the forest, but in a new trend. Few will renounce their power tools; none would choose a quaint old crosscut saw in preference to a flashy Husqvarna. But it is as true today as it was a century ago: "He who uses wood is warmed twice, once in the getting, and later in the burning."

And Drawers of Water

*I*n 1887, when my Father pre-empted his 164 acres, of Lot 16, Cowichan Lake, and first built his small log cabin near the river, he was obliged to lead what in those times was considered a most primitive existence. This was as much a matter of necessity as of choice for money was scarce indeed, and though in the cities jobs were plentiful wages were pitifully small. He was much attracted to a life in the country, however, and I do not think that privations and substitutes concerned him greatly.

Firewood was as close as the nearest tree, there were fish in abundance in the lake and the river, deer and grouse in the forest. Water was carried by bucket or pitcher from the nearby creek or else from the river. (This, of course, was a lifetime removed from the day when the sinister word "pollution" became a commonplace; the creek flowed throughout the year, whereas now it becomes dry by early June and remains so until the fall rains begin again. And now, the village water supply is chlorinated, and in the sultry days of mid-August, there may be days when one might hesitate to swim in the sludgy waters of the river.)

I do not know when my father installed the first hand pump to lift water from the river, but I think it may have been in 1911 or early 1912. At that time, a small fire destroyed the kitchen of the log house and threatened the rest of the building, and my mother used to tell of racing down to the river to fetch pails of water to throw on the blazing shingles. This indicates, I feel, that the hand pump was not functioning at that time.

Such necessary activities as gathering firewood and pumping water are essential parts of frontier life at Greendale estate on the Cowichan River.

There are several efficient types of hand pumps; there is the wing pump, which takes up but little space, there is the force pump, designed to lift water to an impressive height, and then there is the old-fashioned pitcher pump that one encounters in museum replicas of old farm kitchens, and it is the original Myers Pitcher Pump that I associate with the scullery of the old house. It was positioned to the right of the sink beside the high window and to this very day, "the inward eye, that is the bliss of solitude" (according to poet William Wordsworth) envisions the old pump, painted dark red, with its long curving handle, and the inner ear recalls vividly the creaks, the groans, the splutterings and strangled coughings that ensued before water finally gushed from the spout in a steady stream.

Those whose homes were equipped with pitcher pumps spoke knowledgably of "prime" with comments like, "The pump lost its prime," or "You have to keep on priming," or "*Our* pump always holds its prime". These phrases are unintelligible to the city-dweller but if a house is situated at some distance from the water source — be it well or lake or river — the pump must be primed before it will lift. And priming consisted of pouring water, jugful by jugful, with one hand, into the yawning throat, and pumping the handle vigorously up and down with the other. Now and then, my father would speak darkly of the need for a check-valve that would hold the prime, or of a foot-valve attached to the intake pipe at the river, but this was wishful thinking, and during its reign the Myers Pitcher Pump must have required priming no less than 10,000 times!

When at long last, it was dispossessed by the gravity system decades ago, it did not achieve a hallowed resting place, for to the best of my knowledge, it was unceremoniously cast aside in a communal dumping-ground, somewhere near the foot of Hill 60.

The wheels of progress revolve slowly but inexorably, and in time, my parents began to feel that a better water-system was necessary. Pumping water from the river by hand was time consuming, and even though a large oaken barrel had been set up in the scullery, it, too, had to be refilled from time to time, and scrubbed out now and again. In these far-off pioneer days actual cash was always scarce so there was no thought of a brand-new gravity system.

In the end, through the influence of a somewhat raffish and none-too-clean junkman, my father purchased an old gasoline engine manufactured by the Aermotor Company of Chicago, and an aging gear-pump. I am ill-informed concerning the Aermotor Company; I do know, however, that among other products they turned out hundreds of metal windmills, several of which were installed on the lakeshore properties of certain of the earlier settlers. One of these still exists at the March Farm, at Honeymoon Bay, and though inoperative has become a landmark and a legend. Perhaps the fact that our old Aermotor engine was air-cooled explains the name, or perhaps the company was more successful with the windmills and abandoned the engines. So far as I know, I have seen only one other gasoline Aermotor, and that had been installed a lifetime ago at the Stoker property near Marble Bay. Where it may be now I cannot say.

The Aermotor and the primitive pump were merely the beginning of the new regime, for equally important was a 500-gallon gravity tank, constructed of redwood slats, held together by five steel hoops, mounted on a high tower or stand and from the platform an intake pipe connected the pump and a discharge pipe to the cold water tap above the sink in the scullery. On the bank above the river a rough shed was built to house the Aermotor and the pump. Most of this construction work was done by a Mr. Bayliss, by no means the most efficient of carpenters, and by my father, in what free time remained when the farm chores were done.

In contrast to this primitive set-up, the splendid Dunsmuir estate downstream boasted a brand-new Fairbanks-Morse engine and pump and a 5,000-gallon tank, as well as a Delco-Light plant. (This, however, was not real pioneering, which consists basically of trial and error, of substitutions, or doing without.)

It was in 1927, I think, when our gravity system became a reality, but I was away at school in Victoria when the installation was done. My father had by then come to terms or more accurately to an armed neutrality with the Internal Combustion Engine, through his association with the Li'l Husky dragsaw, but he was never at ease, or comfortable with any sort of motor. This I could appreciate when it involved the Aermotor, which soon proved to be treacherous, aggressive, unpredictable, and stubborn by turns. Early in the game, I learned to approach it with dread, since it was only too likely to kick back when being cranked, when a broken wrist might be the result.

I think that Father was only too pleased to turn the Aermotor over to me when I was at home for school holidays, and I was eager to assume responsibilities. But each day, I would watch with dismay as the gauge on the new redwood tank fell lower to indicate that it was time once more to refill, and that meant another dreaded session with the Aermotor. I can see it, as I write: a spidery-looking, evil monster, lying in wait to kick back and break an innocent wrist or damage a thumb. Its rhythms, too, were un-nerving; when at long last it had unwillingly started, it did not run with a smooth and even beat, for it was governed by what was known as the make-and-break system of ignition. This meant that as the flywheel revolved, faster and faster, it reached a point where centrifugal force intervened, and a type of governor took control, to slow the motor down. This was colloquially termed the make-and-break ignition system, and explains the syncopation of the firing. The Aermotor, as I have suggested, did not run with a regular "pop-pop-pop-pop", but rather with like this: "pop--pop--pop-pop--pop-pop---pop-pop-pop-pop-pop." And when, as frequently happened, the muffler had been removed, the shattering explosions could be heard far, far away.

In our ignorance of things mechanical, my father and I did not know that a simple adjustment of the spark control would have prevented, once-and-for-all, the fear of backfiring, and so, for the several years that followed, we were never really at peace with the Aermotor, for the thought of fractured wrist or a damaged thumb was ever-present.

And thus, once more, the winds of change began to stir, and it seemed time for yet another phase of progress. The Aermotor, in all truth, had not been a faithful servant. It was temperamental, it sulked, and when out of commission, it became necessary to fill the redwood tank by hand, a slow and laborious process, to say the least. At such times, some of our more energetic guests would muster for Pumping Duty, and tugged with a will at the wooden handle connecting with the pump. But generally 50 strokes later, they were exhausted, and usually drifted away to more leisurely pursuits, while the Aermotor appeared to gloat in the background.

One day, my father noticed in the *Cowichan Leader* that a Fairbanks-Morse Water System was for sale at the Duncan premises of Tom Pitt, (the Chevrolet dealer). Pitt was widely known and respected, my father knew him well, and believed him to be incapable of shady dealings. Therefore, a few days later, we were the proud owners of yet another internal combustion engine. It is true that the Fairbanks-Morse system was not in its first flush of youth; in fact, upon referring to the tattered instruction manual, we learned that it was a one-and-a-half horsepower model, known as the "Jack Junior", and that it was all of 25 years old! Still, it was a great improvement over the Aermotor. It was furnished with a double flywheel, a more sophisticated make-and-break ignition system, a few brass embellishments, and when finally in operation, it seemed almost silent when compared to the ear-shattering explosions of the Aermotor.

The pump, too, was a massive thing, with a huge air chamber, and the piston, as it travelled back and forth, discharged impressive volumes of water in a steady stream. A wide canvas belt connected pump to engine, and could be adjusted as necessary. The local garage man (George Johnson) and his brother Chappie installed the system, which required a larger engine house and a sturdy slab of 8' by 12' fir upon which the unit was mounted. All this took several days, but finally, the Fairbanks-Morse Jack Junior, revitalized with new batteries and spark plug, replete with gasoline and lubricating oil, responded to a quick turn of the crank handle, and presently a steady stream of water flowed into the redwood tank. The Johnson brothers beamed with pride, as well they might, and my father with relief, for we were assured that whatever else might transpire, the Jack Junior could never kick back.

And so began a new and relatively trouble-free era; the Fairbanks-Morse served us faithfully and well over many years. Seldom did it falter, and when it did minor adjustments restored it to life once again. Its activities depended upon the season of the year; in winter, it was operated perhaps once a week, in the heat of summer, when garden and lawns desperately needed watering, perhaps twice a day. And by now, the Greens had allowed themselves

Alfred Green, above, who was married to notorious Aunt Doll, fell during the brutal fighting of the Great War.

to become more civilized, with the advent of a three-piece bathroom, not, it must be stated, in the tradition of a Dunsmuir bathroom, but a modest, practical one. (At this point, I recall that an elderly lady, one of the habitués of our small guesthouse, upon meeting a friend recently returned from Greendale to Victoria, remarked "I *hear* the Greens have had a bathroom installed, but DOES IT WORK?") Well, it *did* work and has continued to work, despite various ups-and-downs, over many a year.

PART II

Greendale Times

CHAPTER THREE

Who's Who and What's What

Aunt Doll's House

Aunt Doll's house was located east of my parents' house, perhaps a half mile downstream, high on a treed hill. If you looked closely through the dense forest you'd get glimpses of the Cowichan River far below.

It was built of cedar logs, chinked with moss, and the roof was made of split cedar shakes. The sitting room window was on one side of the door and the bedroom window on the other. At the back of the house was the lean-to kitchen, woodshed and a store room where Aunt Doll kept her empty jars and boxes.

Her flower garden consisted of asters in boxes and nasturtiums, but mostly she didn't bother. She liked things that didn't need much looking after; and anyway, in the summer there wasn't any water for the garden.

The white briar rose grew at one end of the verandah and even climbed up over the roof. And the red currant bush was trained against the sitting room wall and smelt lovely in the spring. There had been cowslips and primroses, too, but they died after a while and Aunt Doll didn't bother to plant any more.

When it was summer the string hammock was hung on one end of the verandah and on the top steps there was a box with the hens and chickens plants in it. They had grown out all over the side of the box and Aunt Doll said they only flower once in a hundred years so she didn't know what colour the flowers would be. But in the winter the hens and chickens were on the pantry ledge and the hammock was rolled up in the attic.

The door was always open when the sun shone, but in the winter we knocked and Aunt Doll would call out, "Come in, boys." She would be sitting at the table drinking tea and smoking a cigarette and she would laugh a lot and ask how school was going, and give me the funnies she had saved out of the paper for me.

Sometimes she and Brian would play cards and we could play the gramophone if Aunt Doll wound it. There were a lot of records, too, thick heavy ones with the name Columbia on them. Some of them we knew off by heart: "Three O'clock in the Morning", "The Sheik of Araby", "Dear Old Pal of Mine", and "The Girl who Smiles". Aunt Doll always liked that one but I liked "Selections from Carmen" and "Cavalleria Rusticana" better. Then there were a lot of big, thick records with a rooster on the label, but Aunt Doll never played those because she had lost the diamond needle and you couldn't use the other kind.

When we had played enough records we could look at the pictures on the walls. There were a lot of pictures and photographs, too. There was a painting of the sea breaking over some rocks, away up the west coast. Aunt Doll had painted that years ago and she had painted the pansies in the blue bowl and the red poppies, too.

Then there was a photograph of Aunt Doll, and Aunt Kitty, and Aunt Nan all together wearing funny clothes and another one of a lady with a sailor hat on and a lot of hair underneath. She had written her name in the corner, too. "To dear old Doll, with love from Ethel Jaynes". (Aunt Doll said she was an actress and lived on the stage but no one knew where she lived now.)

And there was just a small picture of Uncle Alf in his uniform. He had been killed in the war and Aunt Doll never talked about him either, because once when I was smaller I had asked Aunt Doll who the soldier in the picture was, and she had said, in a funny, cracked voice "Don't you know who that is? That's your Uncle Alf" and I got all hot and red and talked about something else. I thought I could just remember Uncle Alf the day he went away. He was tall and was wearing his uniform and saw me playing behind the chicken-house. He took me up in his arms and said "Goodbye," quickly and then went out of the gate and down the road and I never saw him again.

Sometimes when Brian got tired of playing cards he would get down the Kipling books from the shelf and read *Rikki-Tikki-Tavi* or *The Jungle Book* stories to me. He said he wanted to read all the books someday and Aunt Doll would let him take them home one at a time. Once he asked if she would leave him the books in her will and she laughed a lot and told him that she would. I wanted her to leave me something, too, but the gramophone was too heavy and the

As this picture of Frank Green's sisters shows, late Victorian and Edwardian ladies didn't sacrifice their love of fashion when they visited Lake Cowichan.

sewing machine was broken. So Aunt Doll promised me a pocket camera after she was dead.

Aunt Doll always had something for me to eat but she didn't have a cow so I had water or tea instead of milk. Sometimes there were just rock-cakes or cookies, but nearly always there was a chocolate layer cake with three layers and icing all over the sides, too, or maybe a layer cake with white icing. (I liked that kind best.)

In the summer I could eat outside on the verandah and watch the big black and yellow swallowtail butterflies, flying in the pinks and red columbines or hear the bees in the white briar roses. And I could rock in the string hammock and hear Brian playing "The Girl who Smiles" or "Dardanella" on the gramophone or reading aloud to Aunt Doll inside the house. And then it would be time to go and Aunt Doll promised to have a chocolate cake next Saturday, and if I had come alone, she would walk down the trail with me to see if the snake had come back again.

I didn't know why my parents didn't want me to go to Aunt Doll's on Saturdays and she hardly ever came to see them. Sometimes, the mailman got the letters mixed and mom got Aunt Doll's, or the other way around, and I would take them back. Aunt Doll smoked a lot and played whist and poker, so perhaps that was why they didn't like her. But it was funny sometimes; Brian thought so, too. Aunt Doll would promise to have a layer cake on Saturday, but then the door would be locked and the blinds and curtains drawn tight over the bedroom windows. I would knock and knock and sometimes call to her but she never came. I knew she couldn't be away or even if she had been very sick she could have at least looked out of her window and told me so.

Sometimes on Sundays I saw Jeff Thorsen's car in the gravel pit down on the road close to the trail. And that was funny, too, because Jeff Thorsen lived in Victoria and had a good job and made lots of money and his wife and children lived there, too. Why would his car be in the gravel pit near Aunt Doll's trail? I didn't like to ask her, somehow, and she never told me why the house was locked up and she hadn't even answered the door when I knocked. She always had an extra nice cake for me so I couldn't ask her very well.

Then one winter, when Aunt Doll had gone to Victoria to take a job, my parents had said one day that perhaps the snow was too heavy on Doll's roof and maybe we ought to go and see. The roof was all right after all. But while Brian and I tried the doors and windows to see if it was locked up tight, Mom and Dad sat on the top step and I just overheard Mom say, "Poor old Alf, buried over there in France. He'd turn over in his grave if he knew what was going on here now!" and then dad saying something about "what might have been." And right after that Brian came round the corner and they got up and said it was time to go home and feed the cows.

Aunt Doll was nice to look at. She had white shiny teeth, and smiled and laughed a lot. She always had nice clean kitchen dresses and a lot of party clothes. Her hair was curly and black with just a little bit of gray on top. Sometimes you would see her talking and laughing with men outside the post office and people would stop to look at her because she was so pretty. The other ladies in the village talked about her behind her back, but they liked her, too, and always asked her to their bridge and whist parties because she played so well and didn't mind losing.

Aunt Doll's bedroom was cold and dark and I didn't go in there very often. There was just the white iron double bed, and a little dressing table, and a pale green clothes closet. The windows looked out into the woods where a little trail went down to the creek. Aunt Doll had planted lady slippers and foxglove beside the path and it was nice and cool there on hot days. There was the attic too, but we had to pull up a trapdoor in the ceiling to get there. The stairs went almost straight up, like a ladder. Up in the attic there were some wooden boxes of old magazines and books, an old bedspring and two brass coal-oil lamps with red and blue roses painted on the china shades. Sometimes Aunt Doll would go up into the attic with me and see if mice had got into the books, but they never had.

I've never forgotten one Saturday at Aunt Doll's when I was about 12 years old. Brian had been away at high school for a long time so I was alone. It was a sunny day and there would be lots of flowers out in the garden, and there was sure to be a layer cake for me. But when I got to the trail, Jeff Thorsen's car was there in the gravel pit. At first I almost turned back but then I remembered the cake and funnies, so I kept on up the trail.

And there, around the sharp bend, I saw a lady in a blue dress lying on the bracken. But really I heard her first because she was crying and moaning and saying, over and over, "Oh God help me, oh God help me. Make him come back." Her straw hat had fallen off and her yellow hair straggled all over her face, which was hidden in her hands. I wondered if she were Jeff Thorsen's wife and what I ought to do to help her. But before I could do anything, she sat up and began to feel for her bag for a handkerchief and then she saw me. She didn't stop crying at first but wiped her eyes and nose and straightened her hair while she stared straight at me and I looked back at her, afraid to speak. Then she said, in a hoarse voice, "Are you going up there, too?" and pointed to Aunt Doll's. I nodded and she went on speaking quickly, but stopping to catch her breath once in a while. "You haven't seen me before have you?" and when I said "No," she went on, "You don't know my name and I won't tell you what it is, and I don't know who you are, either. But for your own sake, for God's sake, keep away from her. She's bad all through, she's wicked and cruel. She'll ruin your life in time as she's ruined mine. You're too young to know what I mean but someday you'll understand. You're just a boy, a child, but that won't stop her. Keep away from her before it's too late".

She started to say something else but began to cry again, while I could only stand with my mouth open, watching her. Then she stood up and walked down the trail, slowly with her face in her hands. The handkerchief slipped out of her half-open bag and caught on a spray of salal but I couldn't run after her with it. After a minute or so I heard the car start and back out of the gravel-pit and drive slowly away.

I stood there for a while and wondered what to do, what to say to Aunt Doll. Perhaps I should turn back home. Perhaps the best thing to do was just go on as if nothing had happened, as if

I'd never seen the lady in the blue dress crying in the bracken. So I went on. There were lots of swallowtail butterflies in the red poppies and I could hear a hummingbird in the white briar rose and smell the pinks.

The door was open and I went up the stairs as usual. Aunt Doll wasn't in the house; she was out in the woodshed splitting wood, banging the axe down hard while the wood and kindling flew all around. She stopped when she saw me and straightened up. She had been working hard but her face was white and stiff, and she didn't try to smile. She just said, "Hello Trevie, help me get some of this wood in before you go." I didn't know what to say or what to talk about but I carried in some armloads of wood while Aunt Doll went on chopping. After a while, she said, "Well Trevie, that's enough of that. Let's go in and sit down for a while."

She sat down in the kitchen and began to smoke. She didn't ask how school was going and she forgot to give me the week's funnies which she had folded in a pile and put away for me. At last she sat up straight and said, "Say Trev, did you meet someone on the trail just now, a woman in blue?" I nodded and she said "Well, that was Mrs. Thorsen and I can just about guess what she told you. But you may as soon forget about it because you won't see her back here again, not after what I told her. Well, you'll hear the same sort of talk about me when you get older. But don't worry over it; I don't. But I wouldn't tell mom and dad if I was you, they wouldn't understand. Now let's forget it. You pack in another load of wood and I'll get the cake out and put on some music. What would you like, "Humoresque"? Might as well laugh while you are young, I say."

The cake was better than ever and Aunt Doll played a lot of records for me, but she forgot to give me the funnies and on the trail going home I saw Mrs. Thorsen's handkerchief. I picked it up; it was thin and had a lace edging and smelled of violets. It wouldn't do to let Aunt Doll see it there so I hid it in the thorns at the side of the trail.

Of course I didn't tell my mother and father about Mrs. Thorsen but I couldn't forget it somehow. And I didn't go to Aunt Doll's so often, either. There was more to do at home after school for one thing and then I had a bicycle and liked going for rides down the river road and up the mountain trails.

About a year after that Jeff Thorsen was put in jail for stealing a lot of money from the government and another man took his job. People talked a lot about Aunt Doll then and stopped asking her to their teas and card parties. For a while she stayed on at the log house but, when winter came, she went to Victoria to stay with Aunt Kitty and was away for a long time.

Mom and Dad never talked about her at all and I didn't either. But once, when Brian and I were in Victoria for a weekend we saw Aunt Doll on the street all dressed up and walking with Aunt Kitty. They were glad to see us both and talked a lot about the old days and the Saturday mornings long ago. Then they asked us both to go to a picture with them the next night. Brian wasn't very keen to go but in the end we both went. Aunt Doll and Aunt Kitty were very kind and paid for the best seats in the house. The picture was called *The Magician*, and Lon Chaney and Alice Terry were in it. Afterwards we all went to a soda fountain for sundaes and Aunt Kitty said to be sure to call in to see her again next time we came to Victoria. But she forgot all about giving us her address.

Then next year I went to high-school at Victoria for a three year stint and I didn't see Aunt Doll all that time. But I heard that she was back at the old house now and then and that Jeff Thorsen was out of jail and had another job. Mrs. Thorsen had moved to Seattle, a hundred miles off, and had taken the children and opened a boarding-house and was doing very well at it, too.

One Easter holiday, when I was at home, I went up the trail to Aunt Doll's just to see the old place. The acacia tree had grown very tall and covered all one side of the garden. There was a lot of broom growing all up the bank from the railway track too but the gorse bush was dead and had been cut down to the ground. There were a few daffodils but they were small and spindly. The red currant had grown tall and straggly and almost hid the sitting room windows. It was in full bloom and there were lots of hummingbirds around it. The curtains were drawn right across the windows and there was a padlock on the door. The kitchen stovepipe had blown off the roof and lay on the porch. Aunt Doll must have been away a long time. She had asked old John Powel to look after the house so Mom and Dad never went there at all.

Two summers later I saw Aunt Doll for the last time. She and Aunt Kitty had come to stay at the old house for a couple of weeks. They worked hard, cleaning up and scrubbing the floors and washing the windows. The garden was pretty wild by then and most of the flowers had been choked out with grass and blackberries. Aunt Kitty's rheumatism was bad and she had to walk with a stick but she joked and laughed about it. I had forgotten that she wore so many beads and bangles.

Aunt Doll looked just the same. Perhaps her hair was a little bit grayer but she wore it just the same way. She had had her teeth out but the false ones looked very nice and you'd never have known they weren't her own. They said that next year they were coming back for all summer and that town life was all right but you got tired of it, too, after a while. They asked if I would keep an eye on the roof if the snow got too heavy because Powel was too old for hard work like shoveling. Then Aunt Doll said, "Goodbye" and that she'd see me in the summer.

Just after New Year mom showed me the notice of Aunt Doll's death in the paper. [Note: date of death December 31, 1937] It said, "suddenly at the home of her sister, in Victoria". I couldn't believe it at first. Aunt Doll was strong and sure of herself; she laughed at illness and death. People like Aunt Doll couldn't die like that. I didn't go to the funeral but Mom sent some flowers. They said afterwards that Aunt Doll looked so peaceful in her coffin. She was dressed in her new black dress with red roses at the waist. They said she might have been asleep.

Two years after that Aunt Kitty died, too. Her rheumatism got worse and worse and, after Aunt Doll had gone, she wasn't the same. She didn't care about anything at all then. She was ill in hospital a long time and never came through an operation.

After that the old log house slowly disappeared. John Powel didn't bother to look after it and no one else cared. First the doors and windows were taken and then the furniture went. One year, the snow was very deep and part of the roof caved in. Then, bit by bit, lumber was taken; one by one the cedar logs were cut up into stove lengths and hauled away. The neighbourhood kids built a shack out of some of the cedar shakes off the roof but in time that fell down, too. So in the end there was nothing left.

The house had gone: the briar rose, the gorse bush, the hens and chickens, the Kipling books, the brass oil lamps. Everything was gone except the acacia, which had grown into a big and spreading tree.

But I knew that as long as I lived I could, when I wanted, turn my mind back to it all. If I shut my eyes and thought for a while, I could find the trail and follow it up to the garden. The sun would always be shining; the bees would be buzzing in the acacia tree. Then two big swallowtail butterflies would come sailing across the red poppies. The box of hen and chickens would be there on the top step and the front door would be open. The gramophone would be playing "Humoresque" and Aunt Doll would be in the kitchen smoking. The layer cake would be in the cupboard and Brian would be reading from Kipling. And I didn't have to think of all that had happened since. I could take a book from the shelf and go outside and lie in the string hammock. If I could I would have let time stop there so that the years ahead, with their worries, trouble, and sorrow, would never come.

Ellen

"Too many cooks," they say, spoil the broth," but one indifferent cook, unaided, can also spoil a great deal of broth. This is the Chronicle of Ellen, who ranks foremost in my memory among a lengthy list of broth spoilers.

She applied, in an untidy scrawl, to my mother's desperate appeal (per the help wanted ads) for a competent cook to take charge of the kitchen during the spring fishing season. A rendezvous was arranged at Duncan, 20 miles away. Thence Mother journeyed by bus with a hopeful heart.

We were somewhat mystified by her attitude when she returned. "What's she like?" was our question. "Well, she's very fat," said Mother, doubtfully. (This, we felt, boded well; fat cooks are usually possessed of good tempers.) "But she's a Cockney, and drops all her aitches," she continued. (This, of course, could be overlooked and ought not to be held against Ellen's culinary prestige.) In the course of the interview, it transpired that Ellen had been out from London for four years and had, during her career, cooked for the Baron de Rothschild, and favored the idea of a Quiet Life in the Country.

"Wull, Oi 'opes Oi'll please yer, Oi'm sure," were Ellen's parting words, as she had lumbered away to catch her train to Victoria. It was a vain hope, from the start.

I was at school the afternoon of Ellen's arrival, but hurried home to meet the self-styled paragon. Mother greeted me with an air of false heartiness. "Come out and meet Ellen," she said brightly. Already, the kitchen was pervaded with the atmosphere of gloom and truculence that ultimately became associated with Ellen. And there was Ellen herself: a vast bulky shape, swaddled in a capacious apron, with a dish towel stuffed in the waistband. "This is Miss Langton," said Mother cheerfully, "But we're going to call her Ellen." Ellen turned ponderously from the stove, and gave me a critical scrutiny. Her grey eyes behind her thick, gold-rimmed glasses blinked stolidly, her thin lips compressed themselves tighter. "'Allow," she remarked and returned to her frying-pan.

Ellen joined us, albeit unwillingly, at supper that first night. Her conversational powers were restricted to "Yus" and "Now" and Mother's efforts to be entertaining and cheerful proved futile. From then on, our cosy, hospitable kitchen became a sinister background for her activities. There, countless roasts were transformed from a wholesome raw state to blackened, leathery carrion. The greasy, doughy suet puddings, relished by the de Rothschilds, she created at the kitchen table. "Beef olives", another of her chef d'oeuvres, consisted of burnt, stringy slices of beef, stuffed with onion, and rolled in breadcrumbs.

[Editor's note: A peep into *Mrs. Beeton's Everyday Cookery* of that period shows a recipe that should have been delicious.]

Imagination and variety were wholly lacking from Ellen's daily menu, but there were always "beef olives". *A propos* of this, I remember seeing Ellen smile for the first time. I had one evening surfeited on beef olives, and finally began to feel acutely uncomfortable. Ellen regarded my pallor with an air of increasing satisfaction. At last, my qualms were not to be borne, and I fled to the refuge of the rhubarb-patch, where, with much physical distress, I parted with the beef olives. Ellen, watching with interest from the kitchen door, applauded my efforts. "That's raht," she shouted cheerfully. "That's the wye to git rid of it," and in her enthusiasm, she so far forgot herself as to bring me a glass of water, for her, a great concession.

Since I was away at school each day, and avoided contact with Ellen whenever possible, I did not fully appreciate Mother's problem. She did admit, at times, that she thought Ellen was perhaps "a little queer," but she clung to the illusion that it would all turn out right in the end. Unfortunately, it did not.

On sunny spring days, when the apple-trees were a pink foam of scented blossom and the lush, new grass studded with dandelions, Ellen would often depart from the field of battle. Lumbering across the grass to the "drying yard", she would slump down on the ground, with her back against the clothesline post, her massive, black-stockinged legs out thrust, her fat, red hands folded on her lap. Sometimes she would sit thus for two hours or more, while within, the kitchen fire would die out, and the grease congeal on the unwashed dishes. Then she would slowly collect herself, return to the house, relight the fire, and brew a cup of tea, before returning to her duties.

Nevertheless, Ellen had Ideas. She believed, for instance, that the clothes on the drying-line were a sordid and shameful spectacle. "Lowers the look of the plyce," said Ellen. (It did not occur to her that she, herself, was also a contributing factor to the lowering of the look of the plyce.)

Ellen's bedroom was small, and sandwiched between the sitting-room and a passage. While it had access by two doors, Ellen preferred to use the window. It called for a rare degree of judgment and manipulation for her to navigate the small opening but she managed without once getting stuck. Those of our guests who witnessed Ellen's massive stern and bulky legs in their stockings and laced boots disappearing through the window, pronounced themselves greatly entertained. Ellen did not like tobacco-smoke; "It ruined 'er eyes," she said. But she seemed impervious to the dense clouds of blue smoke with which her kitchen was generally filled. Nevertheless, Miss Langton's duplicity was discovered by one of my schoolmates, who witnessed her smoking a cigarette in the village while in animated conversation with the town drunk.

A comic and dramatic incident helped to speed our cook's departure. One fine spring morning, Mother arranged to rinse the family wash in the river, in preference to using Ellen's grease-encrusted sink. She, resting comfortably beneath a large apple-tree, witnessed the preparations, and bestirred herself. "Hoi'll 'elp yer," she grunted, and waddled after Mother, down to the float, where the ritual of the rinsing was to be enacted.

Ellen could not have chosen a more perfect background for her denouement. Wild roses and ninebark tossed luxuriant sprays from the bank, and the air was perfumed by the cottonwoods. Even the phlegmatic lady felt a stirring of appreciation, and stared at the sparkling, clear-flowing stream before her.

Gingerly arraying her bulk upon the edge, she selected a bath towel from the clothesbasket, and leaned forward to immerse it in the pool. Here, the words of *Hamlet* prove opportune. We are told that the mad Ophelia, at the stream of Undine,

"While on the pendant boughs her coronet weeds,

Clambering to hang, an envious sliver broke,

When down her weedy trophies and herself

Fell in the weeping brook".

And even so it was with Ellen. While rinsing languidly, she overbalanced and heaving in with a tremendous splash, her baptism was complete. Although "her clothes spread wide," they were incapable of bearing her up. There is a limit to the endurance of clothes. Nor did she,

"Chant snatches of old tunes, as one incapable of her own distress".

Emerging from the flood, her spectacles pendant from one ear, a wreath of some aquatic plant in her hair, she was a Figure of Vengeance, and her first utterances were an accusation.

"Yer joggled the raft so's Oi'd fall in," she spluttered.

Mother, who controlled her mirth with supreme effort, assisted and consoled the victim, tactfully explaining the accident as the misplacing of excessive weight.

"Anywye, Oi'm soaked through," mourned Ellen, as she hauled herself back upon the raft; "And Oi've rewined me styes." While she was without doubt sodden, her "styes", even when dry, proved so ineffective that their loss could not be honestly regretted. With due solemnity, Mother escorted the rejected mermaid back to the house.

But from then on, Ellen's moods became more taciturn, the roasts more charred, the suet puddings more under-done. At length, a Battle Royal occurred, during which Mother became emboldened to give Ellen notice. Ellen waived the order, and demanded what she termed her "Roights". I listened, upstairs, spellbound, as the sounds of altercation arose, and such phrases as "Got me Roights, same as you, ain't Oi?" and "Thinks yer a duchess, but y'ain't," and "Done me best fer yer, and thet's all the thenks Oi git," trembled on the air. At intervals, the crash of a saucepan-lid, or the slam of the oven door created additional atmosphere. But finally, intimidated by a threat of The Police, Ellen yielded ground, and agreed to depart in peace the next day. The beef olives were especially leathery that night.

After breakfast, garbed in her black coat and boat-shaped brown hat, the gold coins in her ears winking beneath, Ellen lumbered out to the highway to wait for the bus. Since it was delayed, she sat on her suitcase, a picture of vengeance and frustration, her lips clamped tightly, and in her eyes a dangerous glitter. At last the bus arrived, and she was borne away to greener fields.

Several years later, my brother and I were sitting one night in Victoria at the Fort and Douglas corner. All at once we became aware of a massive bulk of malevolence approaching. Yes, it was Ellen beyond a doubt: the same coat and hat, the same gold-rimmed spectacles and trap-like mouth. Turning hastily, we

Louisa Spencer and baby Brian Green photographed in 1911.

assumed a hearty absorption in the shop window until Miss Langton had passed by. Some months after this episode, I read in the paper of the deportation from Victoria, as an undesirable character, of one Ellen Langton.

If, and when, I encounter the Baron de Rothschild, (the possibility of which is admittedly remote), I shall exclaim, "Ah, yes, my dear Baron, enchanted indeed to meet you, and I believe that we share a bond of common interest. We once employed your cook."

Estelle

*F*or many years her picture hung on the wall of our little sitting room. At last it was put away in a box, along with many other discarded photographs. But at rare intervals, it re-appears, and once again we see the sweet, rather wistful face, and read the inscription in the lower corner, written in her firm hand, "To Mrs. Frank Green, and Family, Cordially and sincerely yours, Estelle."

And I never fail to wonder if we shall ever know the end of her story. There are other pictures of her, too, and these are large, sepia "chromos", such as might be seen on the billboards in front of the second-rate Vaudeville theatres two or three decades ago. One of these depicts her standing before an open grand piano, the fingers of one slim hand lightly touching the keys. Her high-waisted gown, lavishly trimmed with sequins and bordered with white fur, makes her look incredibly tall and slim; the expression of the face is serious, a little wistful. Another shows her seated on the piano bench, knees crossed, hands clasped, and a winsome, roguish smile lurking at her mouth.

Many years ago, at the end of the Great War, the first meeting with Estelle C. occurred in this manner. One glorious summer day, my parents had taken my elder brother and me (we were very small boys then) for a picnic some distance up the lakeshore. We had moored the boat at a small clearing, called Craig's Landing, a charmingly wooded spot, which adjoined the old wagon trail leading to the North Arm. At this time, it was a delightfully quiet and secluded spot where, for days on end, no one passed; now it is changed beyond recognition. A prosperous auto-camp has encircled Craig's Landing, and innumerable cars and motor-trucks drive up and down the old wagon trail, now a wide, tarred highway. But on this day, we were completely alone, and were preparing to unpack our picnic lunch when through the low bushes that bordered the road came the prettiest lady imaginable. She was dressed in a blue cotton frock, and wore a pink sunbonnet over her golden hair; in one hand she carried an empty pail. In a spot where the isolation was complete, the approach of any stranger would have been startling, but this radiant vision, appearing from nowhere, was a surprise indeed.

She came across to us, and asked in the most charming way, "Can you tell me where a Mr. Frank Green lives?" On being told that she was addressing none other than the Frank Green family, she sat down with us, and in the friendliest, most natural manner, began to tell us about herself. She was, she said, an American actress who, having completed a long series of Vaudeville engagements in the States, had come to Lake Cowichan to rest and relax before returning to the stage in the fall.

She and her husband had bought a small houseboat, which was anchored a short distance farther along the lakeshore, and someone had told her of a Mr. Green, who lived in the village, and who kept a cow. And she was on her way to buy some buttermilk, which she used as a beauty aid. And now she had found the Green family having a picnic in the woods, and so she need go no farther. We listened in fascination to the pretty lady, and to her quaint American accent. My brother and I did not know what an actress was, and the word American was new to us also but we decided then and there that if she were an American, we were very partial to the race.

Before she left, it was arranged that she should visit us several days later, should be given the buttermilk, and be driven home later by my father with the old horse and buggy. My brother and I were sick with impatience until the appointed day arrived but at last it came, and during the afternoon, the lady made her way through the maze of stumps and shoddy outbuildings that cluttered our yard, and knocked at our door. This time, she wore a cherry-red jacket over a white blouse and skirt. The pink sunbonnet was replaced by a red-and-white crocheted hat. She could have worn sackcloth and ashes and have been certain of the approval of two small, admiring youngsters.

The afternoon passed very quickly; the pretty lady played with us, sang to us, and showed us amazing things that could be done with an ordinary pocket-handkerchief. For instance, by deft diagonal folds, and a quick gesture, she produced a hammock, with two babies, side by side, as neat as you please! And again, a quick folding and knotting, and there was a mouse, as large as life, for all the world to see. All too soon, the visit was over, and our pretty lady climbed into the old buggy, holding her tin pail of buttermilk, to be driven the four miles back to Craig's Landing.

Perhaps these first meetings impressed themselves more clearly on my childish mind, but I cannot now recollect that we saw Estelle many times afterwards. Once, however, while waiting at the dirty, drab station-yard for the arrival of the passenger-train, I heard a man's voice beside me say, "Here comes that actress-woman again," and there, across the grimy platform came our pretty lady. Once again she wore the sunbonnet and the blue cotton dress, and it seemed to me that somehow the sun shone a little brighter, and that the station-yard was not quite such a black, dirty spot, because she was there, too!

Even in the enlightened days of the 1920s, there was, somehow, associated with the name "actress" a sinister air of glamor and impropriety. There were those in the little village who cast suspicious glances at Estelle's pretty face and clothes, and who shook their heads over the little houseboat tucked away on the lakeshore. But we were too young to know of such insinuations. It was enough to know that she was always sweet, kind, and charming to two small boys.

Shortly after this, we heard that Jack, her husband, had reached the Lake from a Vaudeville circuit in Seattle. I can barely remember seeing him, but my mother tells me that he was all that was cheap, flashy, and common. As a result of an accident on horseback, he was lame, and limped with the aid of a stick. Gaudy neckties, showy jewelry, and bright yellow shoes, all helped to complete the picture of the second-rate actor. He must have persuaded Estelle to return to the stage at this time, because she asked my mother if personal possessions at the houseboat could be stored with us until she might notify us of a permanent address. Mother was very willing, especially as the effects included Estelle's little piano, which was a prize indeed.

So one day, the horse and cart made an excursion to Craig's Landing, and returned laden with plunder. What an afternoon of excitement followed, as my brother and I rooted among the treasures. In addition to the small piano, there were several grass chairs, a deer's head, and a cougar-skin rug, two brightly hued Navajo blankets, a box of books, and a guitar, which, though damaged, could on occasion evoke a few strange, hollow sounds. But what fascinated me most was a tiny model spinning-wheel, intricately carved in wood. A pair of snowshoes, and a small cloisonné vase containing some faded paper flowers, completed the collection, except for two large, iron-bound chests, with the initials, "E. C." studded in rivets on the lids.

How our little room glowed when these treasures were assembled! The deer's head, flanked by the snowshoes, hung above the fireplace, the cougar-skin covered one wall, and the Navajo rugs made a cheery glow in a far corner. And on the mantle stood the tiny spinning-wheel, and the little vase. Perhaps the piano afforded the greatest pleasure, for with it we were taught the first rudiments of music by my mother, who herself derived much joy from practising Estelle's difficult classical music and Vaudeville ballads. These included the charming Grace Wazall songs, so popular at that time, and also a fair selection of the ragtime that was being sung and played across the States.

Before her departure, Estelle told my mother that, in all likelihood, her husband would turn up, sooner or later, and demand that he be allowed to claim her possessions. But we were on no account to relinquish them; they were Estelle's personal property, and we were to keep them till she asked for them. In this she was correct, for Jack did appear one day, and asked for the keys to his wife's boxes. However, when my father refused, he made no protest and soon afterwards went and we never saw him again.

After this incident, many months went by, although an occasional short note came from Estelle. Usually, her address was in care of Byer's Opera House, Fort Worth, Texas but her movements were uncertain, owing to various theatrical engagements in travelling stock companies. At last, however, came a more definite letter. She had left Jack for good, and was returning to her old home in Detroit. Would we send all her things to an enclosed address? The piano and grass chairs she did not want. Would Mrs. Green accept them as an expression of gratitude and sincere friendship? So the borrowed trophies were stored away in the two large, metal-bound boxes: the books, the deer's head, and the brilliant rugs, the guitar, the cloisonné vase and the spinning-wheel. Our little room looked bare and drab when stripped of its finery, but there were the chairs, and the little piano after all. And in an indirect way, whatever knowledge and love of music that my brother and I have developed has been the result of a kindly woman's generous instinct.

Again, a long period elapsed before Estelle's next letter. This time, it was postmarked Chicago, and contained an exciting piece of news. She was to be married to a Spaniard, named Narcisco Almargro. They were deliriously happy, and soon after the wedding, were to sail from New York to Lisbon, Portugal, where she was to meet her husband's family. But she would never forget the happy weeks she had spent at Lake Cowichan, nor Mr. and Mrs. Green and their two little boys, and someday, perhaps, she would return with her husband for a brief visit. Perhaps in time, Mrs. Green would write to her, and tell her all the news of her friends at the Lake. Her address would be Fernando el Catolico, 14 Duplicado, Madrid, Spain.

Almost a year passed before Estelle's next letter arrived in a thin, foreign-looking envelope, with a gaudy stamp. She had never been happier; she loved Madrid, and the Spanish people. The Alhambra Palace at Granada, the Fortress of Alcazar, the bullfights at Seville, the mountain citadel of Andorra: all these she had seen and had greatly appreciated. Her baby son had arrived a month before, and was his parents' pride and joy. They had named him Juan but she would always call him Johnny, and how were the Green family, and everything at Lake Cowichan? She wanted to hear, and why did Mrs. Green not write?

My mother promptly answered Estelle's letter, telling her all the news of our uneventful lives, but again it was nearly a year before a reply came, and this was a heartbroken note. Juan had died during a fever epidemic, and with his death, the sun had gone out of Estelle's life. Madrid was like a prison to her; she was lonely, neglected; the Spanish people were difficult, suspicious. She had only one longing, and that was to return to America, where she would at least feel free. She would return as soon as she could, and alone, if her husband refused to join her. Perhaps she could get into Vaudeville again. She didn't know, and she was too unhappy and heartbroken to care. Her letter ended with, "But why do you not write?"

We never heard from Estelle again. Mother's letters apparently never reached her, or perhaps were intercepted. And so her story is unfinished. Our souvenirs of her are few: the faded photographs, the two shabby wicker chairs. But memories are more enduring: a cache of Grace Wazall songs, a Navajo rug, pink paper flowers in a small vase: these stray impressions serve to reach back many years, to the day when we first saw the pretty lady in the blue dress and pink sunbonnet coming along the wooded path toward our picnic table.

Christmas at Greendale Long Ago

*W*hen I was asked by a valued friend, several weeks ago, to write down memories of my childhood Christmases, I was delighted to participate. But later, I was overtaken by doubts and indecisions; I wondered how anyone could possibly find my gropings into a far distant past of the slightest interest. But later on, after due reflections, I realized that what, to me, may seem dull and ordinary may seem fascinating and perhaps homespun and quaint to the younger generation of today. So I shall try to portray, as vividly as I can, my recollections of the Christmas season at Lake Cowichan, from about 1915 to the late 1920s.

I must begin by explaining that at this time, the village of Lake Cowichan was indeed a small community, a logging community, with various small camps located many miles away along the lakeshore. There were, in order of importance, two hotels, the dominion government fish hatchery, the railway station, a one-room school, and but one small general store. And perhaps 20 or so families were scattered about here and there, some dwelling in floathouses, which were moored to the shore at intervals. My parents lived on the river, perhaps a mile east of the village, and our next-door neighbours were some distance away. When my brother and I walked to school each morning, it was very seldom that we met anyone on the road. And when I add that at the time I first attended school, at the tender age of six, there were exactly 12 children, spread through the eight grades, this will confirm my earlier statement of how small was our village.

But before embarking on the theme of Christmas Day, I should mention the School Christmas Concert, and the fever of preparation that began in late November. Each child was drilled and groomed for this great event. Recitations, songs, and carols were practised and eventually mastered, short plays or skits emerged, for which costumes were created by proud and inventive mothers, until finally the great day arrived.

In retrospect, it seems to me, the single classroom was ample and spacious, for not only were there four rows of desks, but the teacher's desk, up front, and the sprawling pot-bellied wood stove, and, at the rear of the building, a narrow cloakroom. Yet when I last entered this school, about 35 years ago, it had shrunk beyond all belief, and how the Christmas tree plus a mob of proud parents could have been squeezed in boggled the imagination. Yet on the day of the concert, there stood the tree, green and majestic, delicately fragrant, and scattered beneath it were sundry gifts, for not only did the school board present every child with a gift, and a mesh bag of "store candy" and assorted nuts, but each of us, by drawing a name from a shoe box, knew to which of his fellow students he must offer a gift.

Of the concerts themselves, I will say nothing. But engraved on my mind forever is the thrill and the excitement of walking up to the school after supper with my parents and my brother, and generally, it seems, in drenching rain, our faithful coal oil lantern providing a feeble glimmer as we splashed through deep puddles or slushy snow.

Yes, these were indeed festive occasions, particularly in later years, when a real flesh-and-blood Santa Claus, attired in a sleazy scarlet suit, with a lumpy off-white mustache and beard, made his first appearance, to stride out on the platform, between the candle and kerosene footlights, to hand out presents to the excited children.

It must have been all of 9 p.m. when the Green family again braved the elements to trudge the long mile home, in the darkness, through the rain and the puddles, yet two small boys trod, as it were, on clouds of glory. The school concert was over, we had not brought disgrace and ruin to the family and henceforth the Christmas holidays stretched blissfully ahead.

But our own Christmas Day at home: precious indeed are these memories, which come flooding back unbidden as clearly as if they had occurred yesterday.

Again, I must stress the isolation of our small log-and-frame home beside the river, and the fact that, by present standards, we were poor indeed. No car, no bicycles, no plumbing nor running water, no telephone, (there were but seven or eight telephones in the village at this time), candles and kerosene lamps in place of electricity, and, let me hasten to add, for the benefit of the jaded youngsters of today, no piano nor phonograph, and of course, no radio or television. Yet how deprived were we, actually? We, as children, had wonderful parents, plenty of good plain food, perfect health, and little reason for envy. Certainly an object lesson of the truth contained in the current phrase: less is more.

But back to the excitement and the preparation of the family Christmas. Apart from the school concert, there were really no other festivities in our village. There was little social visiting among the 15 or 20 families, Duncan was 21 miles distant to be reached only by a twice-weekly passenger train, and in the entire village itself, there *may* have been three privately-owned cars. Therefore, Christmas must needs be a family affair, though for several years, my parents always invited an elderly bachelor named John Powel, to share our feast such as it was. Powel was terribly deaf, and I am sure, was unable to hear my piping and childish voice, but he seemed to enjoy the warmth of my parents' welcome, as much as the bountiful dinner that followed.

Another invited guest was my father's cousin, familiarly known as Uncle Bill, who was truly the Skeleton at the Feast. My mother disliked him intensely, and my brother and I always rejoiced greatly if and when he declined to accept in favor of either a previous invitation, or a hangover. His caustic asides, his gloomy predictions, his sardonic chuckles, did much to extinguish the True Spirit of Christmas, especially when he had snarled out his seasonal greeting: "If anyone wishes *me* a Merry Christmas, they can go to hell." (Small wonder, then, that my brother and I were more than delighted to be told that "Uncle Bill won't be coming this year." His Christmas gift of 25 cents for each of us, we could cheerfully do without, for although it was considered "a lot of money", it was invariably presented with the admonition, "You think you're happy, doncher!")

I do not believe that I am guilty of speaking ill of the dead in my references to Uncle Bill, departed now these many decades. He was a less-pleasant part of the Christmas season, yet he must be included it I am to present a faithful vignette of the Blessed Day.

I remember that my father would venture forth to the surrounding woods to bring back the Christmas tree, usually a day or two in advance of the 25th of December. Sometimes, there would be deep snow. It seems to me now, in retrospect, that a "green Christmas" was unheard of then and much effort was involved in hitching the horse to the sleigh, and plunging off through slush or deep drifts of snow to the forest. But when the tree was brought in to our small living-room, set up in a corner by the fireplace, and festooned with its decorations it was a glorious sight indeed.

The decorations consisted of long ropes and strands of somewhat tarnished tinsel; there were strands of what were called wood-chip garlands as well, colored red or dark green; there were glass icicles; and there were the small metal candle-holders that were clipped on to the tips of the tree branches to hold the pretty spiral wax candles, colored red, yellow, pale blue, green and white. These, when lighted, gave forth a nostalgic aroma of hot melting wax, and this, combined with the fresh spicy perfume of the tree and the pine fronds over the pictures and on the mantel shelf was all a part of the old fashioned Christmas. The tree ornaments were wonderful, made of some strange substance, not china, glass, or metal, yet they glittered and glowed in the candle light in bright colors.

There were balls and prisms, and two strings of small colored bells, there was a most realistic pink rose, and a squirrel, fashioned from tightly wadded cotton-wool, colored dark brown, and clutching a small cone, which had been given to us by a kind German woman, who lived miles away up the lake. There were one or two strange-looking birds, brightly coloured, and sporting brilliant artificial plumage, and all these items shimmered and glistened in the soft light of the candles and the flickering flames from the fireplace.

On Christmas Eve, our long black stockings were hung on either side of the fireplace, to be miraculously stuffed overnight with a wide variety of small gifts. Always, there were the traditional orange at the toe, some nuts, perhaps a candy bar, a pair of home-knitted stockings or mittens, small games or novelties, and usually one or two books. The more conventional presents were arranged beneath the tree and were simply and sparsely wrapped. White tissue-paper was something of a rarity. Broad bright ribbons and colorful Christmas seals had yet to make their appearance. The baneful word "commercialism" barely existed. But the gifts themselves spoke of love and thoughtfulness and sincerity for a family living far-off in the wilds of the Cowichan Valley.

The presents from the pioneer March Family, miles away up the lake, were unvaried from year to year: for my father, a pair of hand-knitted socks; for mother, a lavender sachet; and for the boys, a four-pound jam tin, crammed with homemade peanut brittle, and a "shin plaster" for us each. That was the crude term for the small 25 cent paper bills. A generation has passed since I last saw a shin plaster!

Other gifts consisted of books, card games such as Happy Families, Rook, and Pit, and other games, like Ludo, Halma, Parcheesi, Snakes and Ladders, Tinkertoys, small Meccano sets, jigsaw puzzles, perhaps a clockwork train, and other small mechanical toys. We were too young, at first, for skates and a sled, and what was termed a Road King Coaster wagon appeared some years later. This wagon, ordered through Eaton's Catalogue, came all the way from Winnipeg, by rail, and eventually arrived at our local station. The excitement of fetching the large oblong package, and the joy of assembling the Road King Coaster, (roller-bearings and all!): these details are still amazingly clear to me.

After the ritual of opening the presents beside the open fire, we adjourned to the kitchen-dining-room for the feast, and truly a feast it was. The plum-pudding had been prepared some weeks previously, and now boiled and bubbled in its enamel cooking-pot. Vegetables from our own garden were abundant: good old-fashioned vegetables, such as potatoes, turnips, carrots, or parsnips. A far cry from the "essentials" of today: celery, olives, sliced tomatoes, avocados, and pickles. But we did indeed have a turkey every Christmas, and a few words as to its origins would be in order.

Next door to us, and some distance upstream, was a pretty log cabin, or summer home, owned by a well-to-do Victoria family. My father and his brother had, I believe, hauled in the cedar logs that were used in its construction, and no doubt had split shakes for the roof. The Victoria family spent happy summers, and generally Easters at Cowichan Lake, but at that time, it seemed too far away from the city for "long weekend" interludes, so that we saw little of them from late August until the following April or May. But each year a turkey arrived for us at the railway station, and for many years there were many extras: a box of Japanese oranges, a wooden box of Smyrna figs, another of dates, a large package of cluster raisins, a bag of glowing holly sprays, and books or games for the small boys.

(I must add that the Tradition of the Turkey continues to the present day, an unbroken record for more than 65 years! Few families can boast of a similar record.)

Another Victoria benefactress has been gratefully remembered in a different way. This kind lady had two small daughters, and my father's sister was nurse, or nanny, in the household for some years. Thus we boys fell heir to certain garments: coats, mittens, scarves, and boots, (for children did sometimes wear boots then) that nowadays might be classed as "unisex" items. But early one Christmas morning, my brother Brian and I came downstairs, and were wide-eyed and wonderstruck to see on the kitchen table a small round object or contraption, upon which there revolved a flat greenish disc, from which arose, faintly, what might be termed "strains of unpremeditated art".

This was our first phonograph: a genuine Stewart-Warner, and from it and its collection of "78" 10-inch recordings, our musical lore was developed. Kind Mrs. R. had selected such gems as "The Parade of the Wooden Soldiers", "Christmas Time at Pumpkin Center", "Twinkling Star" (gavotte), "Vamping Rose" (foxtrot), "Johnny's Christmas Dream of Old Mother Goose", and for my father, a 12-inch Red Seal disc of the glorious tenor voice of John McCormack singing "The Irish Emigrant's Lament".

It was from this generous gift, over many years, that our appreciation and understanding of music, classical and not-so-classical, was fostered and developed.

It is true that the Improved Stewart-Warner Phonograph did have its limitations. The spring-driven motor was noisy, the brake failed early in the game, the steel needles had to be changed with every playing, and since the entire machine was made from metal, (though painted to resemble wood veneer) there was a shrill metallic echo in the musical background. But it served us faithfully and well for several years, until supplanted by a more grandiose machine, likewise a table model, that boasted small doors concealing narrow wooden louvres, and flamboyant designs painted in bright colors. By this time, the Stewart-Warner Company had branched out into several fields in addition to producing phonographs; they manufactured speedometers and ammeters for cars, and at one point, they produced a wide range of radios and other electrical gadgets in which realm they still function, I believe.

After Christmas dinner was over, crackers were pulled, glamorous paper hats were adjusted, and mottoes or jokes were read aloud. The crackers of those times were vastly superior to those of today. They were large and brightly colored, and went off with a resounding bang, and each contained not only a hat and a motto, but a toy or a small game as well. Nor did they cost the world, as they do today.

I may have conveyed the impression that Christmas Day was generally dull and wet, or that there was snow lying on the ground outdoors. This was often so, but there were occasions when the sun shone gloriously, the snow sparkled and glittered, faint blue shadows beneath the trees providing contrast, and sometimes crystals of ice danced and sparkled along the river bank. These intervals were known as cold snaps, and might last for several days or even weeks. But again, we got off lightly, as they say, for there were no water lines to freeze, no plumbing to be damaged, no snow tires to be dealt with, no "adverse driving conditions" to be faced. Of course, there were the extra burdens of roofs to be cleared, trails to be shoveled out in heavy snow, and woodpiles to be renewed from time to time.

Boxing Day generally passed uneventfully. There was no door-to-door visiting that I can remember, and New Year's Day somehow seemed a bit of an anticlimax, when compared with Christmas seasons of long ago, when I was a child. Were they better or worse than their present-day counterparts? It is really not for me to say, nor to moralize. Certainly, they were different; they were very simple, perhaps childish in comparison, but they were innocent and happy occasions, and I feel supremely grateful to possess these cherished memories.

Riverside Hotel

I 've spent just about all of my life in and around the village of Lake Cowichan. My dad built his home along the Cowichan River in 1887 and my wife, Yvonne, and I have lived there since 1947.

Up to the time of the First World War, the forests around the lakes and rivers here were basically intact ancient stands.

My father and his brothers built the first Riverside Hotel here in 1886.

The completed Riverside Inn offers significant comfort to anyone willing to make the arduous trip to Lake Cowichan in the Democrat wagon, seen in the foreground.

Besides running this inn, Dad also provided twice-weekly stage service for passengers, mail and freight. The vehicle, known as a Democrat, was drawn by a pair of horses. The trip to Duncan took about four hours. The next day Dad would load up for the four-hour return trip over this rough road between the communities. He ran the inn and the stage for about three years.

Here follows some information on the Democrat from a Kaatza Station Museum display, giving some interesting background on this essential part of life in the village in its early days.

The Democrat stagecoach was built in 1886 and was the essential link between Cowichan Lake and Duncan. Beginning around 1909 it was used to transport the Greens' guests as well as hauling much needed supplies.

It was an eight-passenger stagecoach and used two horses in good weather and four in bad.

Latterly it was used by the Greens for family outings around the lake, as well as serving as a handy way to carry hay and firewood.

The Democrat was retained by the Green family until Frank Green's death in 1947. From then until 1955 it remained in the old barn but in 1955 the Democrat was donated to Gerry Wellburn and in time it became part of the B.C. Forest Museum collection. In 1992 it was given to the Kaatza Historical Society and in 2002 it was loaned to the Green family to be displayed on the property where it first resided nearly a century ago.

Here's the story of a trip, related by stagecoach driver Basil Kier.

"At Robinson's Farm there were two large fir trees with just enough room for the stagecoach to go between, which we called the gateway to Cowichan Lake. Then we stopped at Currie's Creek to water the horses. There was a bucket left there for that purpose. The Sahtlam Hill was long and steep; after passing Jordan's Farm one was in the dense forest all the way to the Lake. At a place called the half-way was an old hotel and stable operated by a Mr. Lee from Duncan and it had been closed for a long time. It was later purchased by W.E. Oliver, was dismantled by Dan Savoie and the logs brought to the lake where they were used in some of the buildings there. That hotel was situated just where the present railway crosses the road before you go up the halfway hill. This was a long, steep hill and when one reached the top he was at the summit.

"From there we drove through dead timber and next came to a place we called 'the slide', about a mile east of Ripp's Road. There had been a slide down the mountain bringing trees in its path to only 15 feet off the road. Here was a tangled mass about 100 feet high. You were in exceptionally beautiful scenery here: a large variety of ferns, mosses, and fine looking trees. Next we stopped at Ripp's watering place. A bucket was always left here for watering the horses. Then soon we came to the river and the journey's end. Make no mistake about it, it was a beautiful trip over the road and it is nothing short of a crime that a mile of that timber, with all of its beauty, was not left standing for everyone to enjoy seeing."

Now back to Trevor's story.

Logging was always the vital activity for our people, and water was very important for local transportation. We travelled in everything from canoes to tugboats. Until the railway came, the river was used for log driving during periods of high water.

The Esquimalt and Nanaimo rail line was extended to our village in 1913. People would travel from their cabins or float camps along the lakes, often by tug, to the village and then by rail to Duncan, Crofton, Chemainus, and other places on the coast. With road improvements later on, passenger rail service died out. For a while we had bus service. I remember one of our lady school teachers who would bicycle to Duncan on Friday to be with her folks, and then back again Monday morning to teach her classes for the rest of the week!

The Cowichan River has always drawn "notable people" for sport fishing of our famous steelhead trout. It was rumored that the Prince of Wales came here to fish in 1918. He is alleged to have stayed at the Riverside Hotel under an assumed name.

Today, the village of Lake Cowichan serves the various needs of its residents as well as those of the forest and recreation industries. It's a good place to live.

Trevor Green has had a close relationship with the Cowichan Lake Research Station of the B.C. Forest Service since its opening in 1929. He was a member of the staff 1964 - 1977, and today serves as custodian on weekends and statutory holidays. Mr. Green participated in the 1991 annual meeting of our Association at the Station where he recounted some of his wonderful experiences to members present.

Bob DeBoo September, 1991

Some Reminiscences of the Dunsmuirs

"*T*hese, then, are a few scattered recollections of the long ago days when the James Dunsmuirs and their family were our next-door-neighbors down the river."
-prepared with the help of the Craigdarroch Castle Historical Museum Society

VICTORIA'S CRAIGDARROCH CASTLE

My first contact with the illustrious Dunsmuir family occurred when, at a tender age, my brother and I had been taken by my mother to visit her cousins, the J.W. Spencers, who lived on Joan Crescent, directly across from the castle.

I remember that we played on the sidewalk with my small cousin, Myfanwy Spencer, under the watchful eye of her French nanny and dominating the background, looming against the sky, was the great castle. Even then, there seemed to be an air of mystery brooding over the edifice: the soaring "pepper-pot" towers, many balconies, and impressive wrought-iron work.

But, most intriguing of all, to my childish mind, was the information that Nobody Lives There Now. It was challenging: why did no one live there now, and where had they gone?

Years later, I visited Craigdarroch with a group of fellow-students from Victoria High School, which was not far distant. Our French teacher had decided that exposure to the living language could best be effected by a lecture in French on the topic of Versailles, presented by one Mme. Sanderson-Mongin. So on a bright and sunny afternoon, we trundled along Fernwood Road, across Fort Street, and past the impressive stone walls and pillars of what had once been the entrance gates to the castle.

I remember not one word of the lecture and Mme. Sanderson-Mongin remains in my mind as a vague and shadowy figure. I seem to recall that the classroom was upstairs, but stripped of its furnishings, and serving in a functional manner as Victoria College. To me, at that time, Craigdarroch Castle seemed bare and forlorn.

Some years ago, I paid a hasty visit, and was gratified to find that some of the lower rooms had been restored, and that an air of dignity and grandeur was evident. I thought, too, how splendid the estate must have been during its early years, with magnificent views in every direction, spacious grounds, stretches of natural woodland, and above all, the privacy that existed in those far-off days.

During my three years of attendance at Victoria High School, my brother and I were often invited to our cousins, the Spencers, and always, there the castle stood across Joan Crescent splendid and majestic, yet somehow aloof from the passing scene. I remember that the stone wall fronting Fort Street extended eastwards almost as far as Carberry Gardens, as well as partway downhill in the direction of Moss Street, but now, no trace of this wall remains.

My recent visit to the castle I found most rewarding in many ways. To see many more rooms splendidly restored, many heirlooms replaced, much of the Dunsmuir family history delineated, and a highly qualified and dedicated staff to receive the many visitors: all this is encouraging, indeed.

BURLEITH HOUSE

In about 1926 or 1927, while I was attending high school in Victoria, I frequently bicycled, on Saturdays and Sundays, to the distant environs of the city. The Gorge and Esquimalt seemed to have a special attraction for me, and one fine afternoon, while prowling about sequestered areas and side streets, I came upon a most imposing but vacant mansion, fronting, I believe, on Selkirk Water.

This, though I knew it not at the time, was Burleith House, owned by the James Dunsmuir family prior to their removal to

Government House, and later, to Hatley Park, and even though in the early stages of neglect and decay, some latent dignity and splendour still remained. As far as I can recall, no Private Property or Trespassers Will Be Prosecuted signs were visible, though, had they been, I would have ignored them entirely, such was my fascination with Burleith House. Therefore, I wandered about what had once been extensive lawns and gardens, I admired the porte-cochere and the turrets, I peered through the windows of the great ballroom. I simply could not understand why any family, be they Dunsmuirs or be they not, could bring themselves to abandon such a princely dwelling.

My aunt, with whom I boarded whilst attending high school, seemed vaguely aware of Burleith House, and believed that at one time it had served as a girls' private school. I do not remember if I paid it a subsequent visit, but I recall that I was saddened and dismayed to learn of its total destruction by fire, some years later, What a splendid heritage home it would have made. It, too, must have been surrounded by extensive grounds, for the formidable stone wall, now breached here and there, follows Craigflower Road for some distance and beside the impressive entrance, the lodge, or gate house, may yet be seen.

THE COWICHAN RIVER ESTATE

During the year 1916 or 1917, my family became aware that transactions were taking place downstream from where we lived at Greendale on the Cowichan River. Formerly, our closest neighbours were Colonel and Mrs. Andrew Haggard, who owned an attractive log cottage that they occupied during the summer months, and from which they retreated to Victoria to spend the winters.

Col. Haggard was a brother of Sir Rider Haggard, whose successful novels, *King Solomon's Mines* and *She* had strong appeal to a wide reading public at that time. Col. Haggard, too, had literary pretensions, and wrote a novel entitled *The Two Worlds*, dealing with the glittering social scene in Victoria, during the early 1900s, contrasted to the peace and tranquility of the pioneer life of Cowichan Lake. He also produced a lengthy manuscript dealing with the history of the French Revolution, though this was never published. Possibly his chief claim to fame was the creating of the Haggard Fly, for he was a tremendously keen fly-fisherman, and to this day, I gather, the Haggard Fly is much in demand among sports fishermen.

The next property east of the Haggards' was owned by the Haggertys of Victoria. There stood an old log cabin, and on a well-fenced portion of the garden, strawberries were grown commercially. And next door to this, and close to the river, Captain and Mrs. Stevenson (nee Marian Dunsmuir) had built a most attractive cottage, which they occupied during the summer months. (I remember that, long ago, my brother and I were invited to the Stevensons for the afternoon, to meet their son, Johnny, and to have tea, at which cocoa, topped with a marshmallow, was served. Mrs. Stevenson remains in my mind as a most kind person; of her husband, I recall nothing, other than that occasionally he would call in at Greendale to ask if he might fly-fish our stretch of the river.)

It was these three properties, then, superbly located on the river, that were incorporated into what became the James Dunsmuir retreat at Cowichan, and remained in possession of the family for more than 20 years. And we, as next-door neighbours, saw much activity and construction during the first few months of ownership. The Stevenson cottage, slightly enlarged, became the guest house, and nearby stood a strange tent-like construction, largely composed of wire-netting, to be known as "the meat safe" and used as sleeping quarters for numerous grandchildren over the years.

On the former Haggerty property, the log cabin became a cow-shed, and a new house was built for the resident caretaker;

the first to fill this position being a Captain Scarfe from Victoria. Mrs. Scarfe very seldom appeared on the scene, but two small Scarfe daughters attended the local school in company with my brother and me. When the Oscar Scarfes moved away, the post was filled by Jack Hatter, his wife, and young son, Jimmie, (now Dr. James Hatter.) Jack Hatter served the Dunsmuirs faithfully and well until the estate was again divided and sold.

The Haggard log house became the main living-quarters. Bedrooms and bathrooms were added, and a wide and spacious verandah surrounded the house on two sides. A cottage for the two maids was built, plus a cabin for the Chinese servant, a garage with sleeping-quarters and a washroom for the handyman, and a separate building for a Delco-Light plant, and a huge tower to support a 5,000 gallon water-tank. Finally, a staff of gardeners arrived from Hatley Park to landscape the grounds; a neat pathway, edged with smooth river stones, and planted with a special strain of forget-me-nots followed the river shore for some distance. I was especially impressed with the color of these: a vivid shade of dark-blue, and I was told that they had originated in the greenhouses at Hatley Park. Rhododendrons, lilacs, laurels, roses, syringe, and white jasmine were planted lavishly, and a plane tree and an eastern oak have survived to this day, as have the rhododendrons, to add their particular charm to the still beautiful property.

The various Dunsmuir homes with which I have become acquainted shared a common feature, this being impressive driveways and entrances. Here, at Cowichan Lake, a neat fence of high wooden boards curved inwards to the metal gate, that was hung between two sturdy gateposts, the tops of which were gracefully curved. As a final touch, the buildings were all painted a dark brown, with a white trim, except for the Jack Hatter house, which was painted green. That house was a replica of several such dwellings that I saw, long ago, at Hatley Park.

The Delco-Light plant serviced the main house, whereas the guest house and the Hatter abode were provided with kerosene or gasoline lamps. A cow provided the family with dairy products, and the caretaker maintained a small but productive vegetable garden.

It was generally considered that Jack Hatter, the caretaker, had a really "soft job", with a salary of $100 per month, free rent, the advantages of the cow and the vegetable patch, a McGregor saw to simplify the maintenance of the fuel supply, and little to do in the winter months, other than snow removal from the overburdened roofs, lighting occasional fires in the guest house and the big house, and starting the lighting plant or the gasoline motor for the pumping system at certain intervals.

I think that Mr. Hatter was aware of his good fortune, though he may have felt some stress during the summer months, when the Dunsmuir grandchildren and their young friends ran riot, and he was known to refer, gloomily, during dreary snowy or rainy days to the estate as "a horrible place in the winter". Eventually, he contrived to purchase a used Model "T" Ford car and he learned, before long, to drive it as far as the village. Eventually, a large tear developed in the canvas top, and on several occasions I have seen poor Mrs. Hatter, seated in the rear, with her umbrella thrust through the rent to protect her from the elements!

My mother made the acquaintance of our new neighbours during their first summer on the Cowichan River, and one afternoon, Mrs. Dunsmuir and her friend, Mrs. F.D. Little, were invited to tea. (In those days, there were few neighbours, and fewer opportunities for friendly gatherings, and thus, the tea hour seemed to be a special interlude for the busy housewives, and their visitors.) My brother and I were posted outside to guide the visitors past various sheds and outbuildings. I remember that we assisted in opening a rather stubborn gate when Mrs. Dunsmuir explained that she was endowed with short arms, so that stubborn gates and doors were sometimes a problem. Mrs. Little I recall as a tall and somewhat formidable person. (Years later, my brother became well-acquainted with her in the financial world, when he was a respected employee of A.E. Ames and Co. He told me once that an elderly colleague at Ames, usually most polite and deferential, referred to Mrs. Little as "that old buzzard". My mother, too, remembered an occasion when she, Mrs. Dunsmuir and Mrs. Little were together, and the conversation turned towards the topic of the future, in terms of stability and security. Mrs. Dunsmuir suggested in passing, in pessimistic terms, that the day might well dawn when the Dunsmuir fortunes could well be at a low ebb, at which Mrs. Little interjected, "Oh, but what would become of US?" as if little else in the world could possibly be of importance!

Later, mother was invited next door to tea, and met Mr. Dunsmuir for the first time; her impressions were of a frustrated and unhappy man, to whom vast wealth had brought little happiness. He seemed to appreciate all that Cowichan might offer as a sort of haven, but referred to Hatley Park as "a filthy hole".

A kindly concern for others expressed by Mrs. Dunsmuir extended to a lonely old man who lived opposite the entrance gate: John Powel, a bachelor, who eked out a bleak existence from his trap lines in the adjacent forests. (I remember him, one morning, offering several racoon skins to my aunt for 25 cents each, and hoping that this would not be a too-exorbitant figure!) Poor John Powel had reason to dread the future that lay ahead. He had no family, no relatives to whom he might appeal, and he knew full well the inevitable limitations of old age and loneliness. It was through her concern and influence that Mrs. Dunsmuir was finally able to arrange his admission to the Mens' Home, on Cadboro Bay Road, for which Powel was deeply grateful.

A group known as the British Israelites was prominent in the late 1920s, and published a bulletin called *The National Message*. I do not know if Mrs. Dunsmuir was a member but now and then my mother received copies of that magazine from her. Their beliefs seemed to centre about certain mystical revelations connected with the Great Pyramid in Egypt, whereby the line of the British monarchy might be traced back to Biblical times. Many and stirring were the "prophecies" expounded by the "B-Is", (as they were termed) especially in the splendid future that lay before the Prince of Wales, later King Edward VIII. His abdication, his fall from grace, and his exile were grave blows to the B-Is, from which I think they failed to wholly recover. One hears little or nothing of them nowadays but I can remember how, from time to time, being approached by an elderly and militant dowager of Duncan, who would ask, "Are you a B-I?," and despairing to learn that I was not.

After the sudden death of Mr. Dunsmuir, in 1920, at Cowichan, while Mrs. Dunsmuir was absent in Seattle, the family continued to make use of their property, generally during the summer months. Occasionally, the guest house might be rented to friends, or used as an overflow for a younger generation. Among those who occupied the guest house over the years were Bishop Schofield (Charles, Columbia) with his wife and family, Capt. McGregor McIntosh and his wife, (nee Peggy McBride) Mrs. Cudemore, (daughter of Mrs. C-C. Gator), and Cdr. and Mrs. Ian Agnew. Twice, I believe, Col. and Mrs. Reginald Chaplin (nee Maude Dunsmuir) spent several weeks at the guest house, and on one occasion, Lady Evelyn Byng, wife of the Governor-General, with her entourage of secretary and gardener, and Jack Chaplin (A.D.C. to the Governor-General) were in residence for several days as guests of Mrs. Dunsmuir. (Baron Byng, meanwhile, had gone to Painter's Lodge, at Campbell River, on a fishing expedition.)

[Editor's Note: This is indeed the famous Lady Byng, who donated the sportsmanship trophy to the National Hockey League.]

Lady Byng was an ardent botanist and a keen gardener, and planned to stock her fine garden at Thorpe le Soken in England, with plants and shrubs from British Columbia. From time to time, we might see the Chaplins strolling up to the village on a fine summer morning, Mrs. Chaplin always charming and gracious, and always fashionably attired.

In subsequent years, we provided the Dunsmuir household with milk, cream, eggs and roasting chickens; I remember a small acid-tongued and hard-featured cook presiding in the kitchen. She seemed totally incapable of producing a smile but later she was supplanted by a Mrs. Bridges type of cook, smiling and warm-hearted. I also remember meeting young Robin Dunsmuir and his elder cousin, James Audain; the former has occasionally since called in at Greendale, to fish, and to reminisce over happy, sunlit days of long ago spent on the Cowichan River.

On one occasion, my mother, staying with her Spencer cousins at Lan Dderwen on Moss Street, was invited to lunch at Hatley Park with Mrs. Dunsmuir and her daughter, Miss Elinor. The Dunsmuir Packard, driven by the chauffeur, provided transportation to and from Colwood, and I believe that mother was awed by the magnificence of Hatley, and charmed by the kindness of her hostesses. I think that her last contact with the family was an invitation to tea next door with Mrs. (Muriel) Wingfield and her friend, Miss Innes Bodwell, who were spending a few days one autumn, or it may have been when Mrs. Robert Droste (formerly Bessie Hope) called in at Greendale to be directed to the premises of Princess Jennie Chikhmatoff (nee Butchart), an acquaintance of long ago days in Victoria.

The following excerpt from a taped interview with a local shopkeeper I feel to be worthy of inclusion at this point.

"When the Dunsmuir girls were staying at the Lake they used to come down every Sunday morning to buy a *Seattle P.-I.* [*Post-Intelligencer* newspaper] from me. In this store we had a counter and a couple of little tables over here where they could eat ice cream, you see, when we had ice cream. And this Sunday morning the girls came in and said: 'Mr. Smith, we want a *Seattle P.-I.* Oh, here it is, right here.' And they gave me two bits. So I took this and I didn't have a cash register, I had a cash drawer, you see, and I pulled it out and I plunked the two bits in and I took a dime out and I rolled it across the doggone counter and they didn't catch it, you see, and it fell onto the floor and rolled over across and the place was kind of haywire built, you know and over by the wall there was a big wide crack, and of course the dime went down the crack. You know those two girls got down on the floor and they tried their dangest to get that dime out of that crack. So I said, "Don't worry about it girls, someday I'll pull it down and I'll find it. Here's another dime." I said, "Money's made round to go around, anyhow." And you know what they said? "Oh no, Mr. Smith, it's made flat to pile up!"

Now back to my own remembrances.

On one occasion, Mrs. Kathleen Humphreys (nee Dunsmuir) with two of her children were invited to spend an afternoon here, to attend a sort of Sports Day, organized by Harry Ross, (father of Ian Ross, of the Butchart Gardens) and his sister-in-law's husband, Will Todd. It was a very informal gathering, on that fine summer afternoon, the small children and the young folk reveling in the water sports down at the river, and joining in some easy going softball or "rounders".

My last contact with Mrs. Humphreys came when I was delivering milk to the guest house; she was interested in what I might divulge of the shattered marriage of Princess Jennie Chikhmatoff and the subsequent gossip with which Victoria was rife at the time. Her summary to all this was, "Well, we all make mistakes," a statement that can apply to all of us in this vale of tears.

Following the death of Mrs. James Dunsmuir, the estate, in the hands of the Royal Trust Company, was again partitioned into the three original properties, the main house, eventually, to be bought by the late Mr. Hugo Beaven of Oak Bay, who seldom appeared on the scene. Since then, the old house has changed hands several times over the years. Now, the three properties are all occupied, and are well cared for, and outwardly have altered little over the past 30 years.

CHAPTER FOUR

Lake Cowichan's 'Characters'

Für Hildegard

More than once, Hildegard has asked me to tell her about the stove in the kitchen of the old house.

I'm talking about the stove that burns sawdust in an age of electrified kitchens; the stove that is lavishly appointed with designs and embellishments; the stove that to my knowledge has produced thousands of meals, under a variety of custodians for well over 50 years.

It's a conversation piece, in short, which has attracted young folk, like flies around a honey-pot, to the old house, to ask politely, "Please, Mrs. Wood, may we see the old stove?"

But somehow, the history has never been revealed. There were interruptions; I would become digressive in my eagerness to leave no detail unmentioned; I would see Hildegard's attention begin to wander, and I would feel frustrated. So now, to you, Hildegard, I dedicate this offering, to prove that, once again, truth is stranger than fiction. And there can be but one title for my effort, "The Old Stove". (How humdrum and commonplace it sounds! But only wait.)

I first saw it very nearly 50 years ago, in a dark gloomy corner of Scholey's General Store, where it had been stored for a few weeks. In spite of stray cobwebs, and patches of recent rust, the nickel trim shone brightly, and the small placard, fastened to the top, read plainly "FOR SALE, $25.00".

It was more than my mother could resist; for years she had cooked on a camp stove, in itself the reverse of a status symbol, and here at last was the chance to buy a kitchen range, (and a "Monarch" at that!) at a price she could just manage to meet. Even father's intense disapproval could not influence her. My father saw no reason why the old camp stove wasn't good enough; it had seen better days, perhaps, but could certainly last a few more years. Why, therefore, encumber the kitchen with a great, heavy, black range that weighed all of 300 pounds, and could not be loaded single-handed into the wagon? And to add to the complications, the only way it could be taken into the house was if a door or window were removed. And so the conflict continued for several days, until finally the horse and wagon lumbered down the driveway with the range, like some juggernaut of old, balanced on top.

A chilly silence pervaded the domestic scene for some days thereafter. Years later, my mother told me that my brother and I sided against her and regarded the new acquisition with cold disapproval, imitating faithfully my father's attitude. This may be so, but after a few years had passed, and the Monarch had exceeded its reputation, it became a part of the household, and even my father's protests were silenced. And still it reigns supreme in the same crowded corner of the old kitchen though the hands that polished it, nurtured it with wood and kindling, removed ashes, and cleaned stovepipes, have long since attained their final rest.

Once, many years ago, it was converted to burn oil, a passing phase that lasted only a year or so due to the rising cost of fuel; next it was converted a second time, to burn sawdust. But years before that, even, came the triumphal day when it was connected to heat water, and the ancient and mysterious coil, or "water jacket", never before used, functioned most efficiently.

Even now, when Hildegard has cleaned and polished the Monarch, it has an air of ancient distinction. The oven door and fire-box, the compartment for kindling and ashes, and the large warming-oven still gleam brightly. On each side of the stovepipe that protrudes from the firebox is a heavily nickeled bracket, or small shelf, to support a tea or coffee-pot; these have an interesting design of five mysterious letters, "M.I.R.Co.", which, when one is properly informed, stand for "Malleable Iron Range Company."

Below the adjustment which alters the grates to burn either "coal" or "wood" is a solid-looking nickeled plate, bearing the number 547, which makes me wonder if Monarch Range No. 546, or 548 could possibly be still in existence? This we shall never know. So much, then, for the outward appearance of the Monarch; of its inner virtues much could be said, but it is enough to add that after 50 years it still fulfills its daily function.

But of far greater local significance was the fact that the appearance of the stove in Scholey's Store gave proof to the report that Mrs. Allan had left the Lake at last, and was Not Coming Back. Rumors and conjectures were rife, and for some days thereafter the topic of conversation between friends or acquaintances would revolve around Mrs. Allan and her family.

So far as I can remember, I saw Mrs. Allan only once, and in retrospect, I seem to see a pale, intense face, framed in a mass of dark hair, as she sat at the piano in our small sitting-room. This was on her last visit to the Lake, when her presence was not welcomed in several homes. I think that even at my tender age, I was vaguely aware of the aura of tension and frustration associated with this strange, passionate woman. Mr. Allan I never saw, and the three children, Jack, Dane, and Pat are less than the most tenuous of memories, but I shall reconstruct as best I can and fill in where necessary in recounting what I know of their story.

The Allan family, wealthy and attractive, arrived in Victoria from Shanghai, towards the latter years of World War One. Mr. Allan had money to invest, and financed the building of the Cadboro Bay Hotel, destroyed years ago by fire. Perhaps it was during their first summer on Vancouver Island that they rented the Colonel Haggard home (Camp Haggard) on the Cowichan River, and arrived with the children and several Chinese servants, thus establishing a standard of living hitherto unknown in the immediate district. Ancient records in an old journal of my father show that he sold milk, eggs, and occasionally cream to the Allans, and that is how the friendship between my mother and Mrs. Allan was founded.

It is possible that at this time the small frame cottage, on North Shore Road, still standing and long the residence of the E. S. Lomas family, was built for the Allans as a summer home. Named "The Shack", it nestled into the woodland growth of cedar and fir, with larger, more massive giants of the forest beyond. How long the Allan family were in occupancy I do not know, but it could not have been for many years.

To condense here, and gloss over facts of which I am unsure, it must be explained that Mr. Allan's business failed; the Cadboro Bay Hotel, possibly due to its remote location in those days, proved to be a fiasco. Whether because of this, or other influences, he and Mrs. Allan drifted apart, he to remain in Victoria to find employment where possible, she to return with the children to The Shack, to live as best they could. From my mother's reminiscences I learned that, through necessity, Mrs. Allan contrived to convert The Shack into a sort of tearoom: a most impractical decision. At this period the only clientele might have been a few gently nurtured guests from the Riverside or the Lakeside hotels; the pioneer stock had no time to sit sipping tea, however daintily served. Gone, of course, were the Chinese servants, in their spotless white, and Mrs. Allan, unused to domestic work, and planning meals, was wholly incompetent. The ice cream, shipped with difficulty and expense from Duncan, melted through lack of refrigeration. And so the rustic tables and dainty chinaware were seldom used even on fine summer afternoons.

Mrs. Allan's background of culture and education in England and Shanghai was totally inadequate in her present position; in fact, if anything, it may have proved a barrier. But she and the three children needed to be fed and clothed and she was not without inspiration. The next scheme, however, was in direct contrast to the tearoom. This time, she posted on a tree near the roadway a sign to advertise her willingness to take in washing for loggers. Even in our far distant part of the Cowichan Valley, nothing could have seemed more degrading, particularly for a woman of the type and social grace of Mrs. Allan. Why she chose to remain at the Lake, why she did not return to Victoria to seek work, I do not know.

How lucrative this enterprise proved to be, again I have no way of knowing. It did, however, serve to further Mrs. Allan's acquaintance with several of the single loggers or bachelors then residing in or about the village. And again there was ample cause for conjecture and for gossip. And certainly it was true that at times the Allan children were shamefully neglected and left alone to manage for themselves, while their mother was away, in company of her new-found friends. She may or may not have possessed the instincts or the philosophy of an Isadora Duncan but it seemed, as time passed, that her moral standards were vastly different from those of her neighbors, to whom the domestic round and the raising of a family were of first importance.

I think that my mother, in recognizing Mrs. Allan's intelligence and background, was able to excuse but not necessarily condone her (at times) unconventional behaviour. But not at all times, for on one occasion they had started for a long walk together, along a seldom-used trail that led through the forest. During the walk, they had discussed many topics: literature, music, art and religion. But later, when they came upon several workmen, busy repairing a bridge, Mrs. Allan, as if compelled by a force over which she had no control, pressed up against one of the grinning men, and said "Kiss me, Eddie!," whereupon Mother, overcome with disgust, turned about, and proceeded homewards alone. When later, on some similar occasion, she felt obliged to remonstrate, to persuade Mrs. Allan to at least consider her children, the response was, "But what can you expect? My mother died of drink, and my father owned a brothel in Shanghai; and I am what I am, rotten all the way through."

But during this interval, Mrs. Allan became infatuated with one of the young loggers, and a hopeless situation developed. Jim Palmer was young, he was handsome, he had charm and a dry humor, but it was unlikely that he felt genuine love for an unstable, intense woman, older than he, encumbered with three children, and his intellectual superior. To her, he was one of Nature's Gentlemen, and in her flights of fancy, she must have envisioned a blissful future, an enchanted life with Jim in the idyllic background of the Cowichan Valley. Perhaps Jim did encourage her to believe in such a future, but he must have felt some relief when at last his strange inamorata yielded to the advice of a sister, who persuaded her to return to England for some months in order to arrive at a firm decision. Accordingly, Mrs. Allan closed up The Shack, sent her son, Jack (aged perhaps 11) to Victoria to live with his father, and departed for England with the two little girls, with all expenses financed by her generous sister. And no doubt the residents of our village sighed with relief believing that a strange chapter had reached its appointed end.

Before a year had passed, however, another situation had arisen. Jim Palmer, encouraged by an equally irresponsible friend, conceived the idea of writing an impassioned letter to Mrs. Allan, urging her to return to the Lake, and hinting that he could no longer live without her. To him and to his friend, Tom Greensmith, it was a harmless joke, and I am sure that they could never have imagined the outcome. But to the poor tormented woman in

England, it was a heaven-sent answer to her prayers. With all possible speed, she returned to Canada, leaving the little girls behind in England at boarding-school fully expecting to marry Jim before many weeks had elapsed. And what of her husband? Again, I am uncertain as to the various intervals of time but I know that for some months he and his son Jack lived in most straitened circumstances in a shabby room at the Ritz Hotel in Victoria, (which even then belied its illustrious name.) When Mr. Allan's failing health developed into an acute illness, and his time was fast running out, Jack delivered papers to pay the rent and provide food for them both. Then, when his father finally died, Jack was rescued by one of the more charitable service clubs, and cared for until his aunt in England arranged that he should return to her for a time.

It is possible that these distressing episodes occurred while Mrs. Allan was yet in England, for I assume that her husband's death would have enabled her to be free to marry Jim Palmer without delay had Jim been willing. But Jim was not willing, and must have been in a state of panic on learning that his proposal of marriage, written in jest, had been accepted in earnest. To give him credit, he did not take refuge in flight when Mrs. Allan returned to the Lake, but his stumbling explanation of his indecision, his playing for time, his change of heart drove the poor wretched woman into a state of frenzy and near-insanity.

The hatred of a Woman Scorned is legendary, and it is not to be wondered at that the village folk were quick to anticipate the worst. Though decades have elapsed since these events transpired, I can still remember vividly our neighbor, Mrs. Keast, (usually placid and unemotional) accompanied by my father's cousin, Bill Swinerton, knocking at our door late one wet night, to warn us that Mrs. Allan was wandering about the village with a loaded revolver, intent on shooting Jim Palmer, and then shooting herself. How much of this may have been exaggerated who can tell, yet at the time it seemed terrifyingly real.

In the end, Jim either made his escape, or else made his peace with Mrs. Allan. Perhaps her love for him was great enough to encompass forgiveness and renunciation, or perhaps she realized that, henceforth, she must begin a new life. At all events, she managed to sell The Shack to the Lomas family, and to sell or part with her few possessions. And that is how my parents came by the old stove.

There were other items, as well, but these were gifts. Several intellectual books were added to my parents' small library; a large music-book, bound in black Morocco, with the name "Jack Allan, 1917" stamped in gold lettering in the lower right-hand corner, provided my brother with his first rudiments for the piano. There were three beautiful plates, brought from Shanghai, supported by thin wire in order to display them on a wall. They glowed and scintillated with gold-leaf and shining glaze, stylized designs of ferocious dragons intertwined with gorgeous butterflies and birds, and the borders were embossed with an intricate pattern of grains of rice. Two other plates, no less beautiful, showed an exquisite tracery of bamboo fronds against a milky background. There were also fragments of a once-splendid nut bowl, beautifully painted with chestnut and filbert leaves, but though the fragments were too large to be cast out, they did not respond to patient applications of "Seccotine" or mucilage. But loveliest of all was a tiny house, a masterpiece of shining lacquer and jewel-like design. The roof of this treasure was made of finely-crushed eggshell, the tiny lattice doors could be opened at need. And below, in what might be considered the foundations, sections could be removed to reveal two small lacquer boxes, one of a glowing, reddish-brown wood, with a golden star gleaming on the lid; the other box, slightly larger, was of glittering black lacquer, with two storks, etched in silver, beside a silver pool. The little house has long since disappeared, the plates more recently. Do you recall seeing them, Hildegard? If they were shattered during your custody of the old house, do not feel embarrassed, but I am sure you would remember their exotic beauty.

But most telling of all, I feel, was a framed picture that still hangs on the dining-room wall of the old house. It depicts, in black and white, a scene of austerity and loneliness. On a snow-covered hillside, in evening light, stands a wolf, gazing far below to where a few snow-covered shacks huddle together. Light is glowing from the windows, but night is descending, and a storm approaches. The wolf, solitary and rejected, is an outcast. Entitled "The Lone Wolf," this picture must have appealed strongly to Mrs. Allan, for in giving it to my mother, she remarked, "I am that wolf!"

Now, a hiatus of months, even a few years, follows. I think that we knew vaguely that Mrs. Allan was working somewhere in Vancouver, and that the three children were either at school in England, or had been sent to Shanghai with yet another aunt. But I remember in precise detail the fine summer day when my mother and I had walked to the village early one morning. On the way home, we stopped at the fish hatchery, at my suggestion, I suppose, to admire Mr. Castley's cheerful flower borders, or else perhaps to look at the fish in the long wooden tanks. And then, before we left, I recall Mrs. Castley leaning from a window with a newspaper in her hand, saying to mother, "Have you seen the paper yet? Mrs. Allan has committed suicide!" I had then no idea what this meant, but it was later explained that Mrs. Allan was dead, and that she had killed herself. Later, months later, I learned that the poor woman, once again "jilted" by the man with whom she had been living, had indeed reached the end of her tormented existence. In a moment of desperation, she had seen her past life as an utter failure, her present as intolerable, and an escape from this world as the only possible future. And so she had carefully locked the doors and windows of her room, stuffed keyholes and apertures with paper or strips of cloth, arranged her children's photographs about her bed, and turned on the gas. Any details of a court enquiry, the testimony of her lover, or her funeral have escaped me.

But the end is not yet.

Years, almost 20 years passed, and the story of the Allans was virtually forgotten. Then one fine autumn afternoon in the early 1940s, I believe, a car approached the house, driven by a tall, dark, fine-looking young man. With him was an attractive young woman, also dark, but of average height. I answered their knock, and by way of introduction, the man said to mother, "Are you Mrs. Green? My name is Jack Allan, and this is my wife, Kae. I used to live here at Lake Cowichan when I was a very small boy, years ago!"

How strange are these meetings, these brief and fleeting contacts, over the years. They are a part of what we call Destiny, but what ordains them, what controls them, who knows? Jack and Kae Allan stayed to tea, and created a most favorable impression. Difficult, indeed, to recognize in this good-looking and poised man the pathetic, delicate boy, caring for his dying father at the Ritz Hotel many years ago. Later, we directed them to The Shack, enlarged and altered since its early days, so that Kae could see the background of Jack's youthful days on Vancouver Island. Although Christmas cards were exchanged for several years, we have not seen them since, but so far as I know, they are still resident in Victoria.

And now comes the final chapter.

About two years after the meeting with Jack and Kae Allan, a letter arrived for my mother, in an unfamiliar hand, postmarked from Victoria. And yet another link with the distant past was revealed, for the letter was from Jack's younger sister, Patricia. She had arrived in Victoria some short time before, had found an office job at the parliament buildings, and was living at the Montrose Apartments on Blanshard Street. She could just remember a Mrs. Green at Cowichan Lake, and was sure that she would be the only person who might have the answers to certain questions concerning Pat's confused and disturbed childhood. Would it, therefore, be possible to arrange a meeting in the near future? She would be most anxious to receive an early reply. Several days after this, I drove my mother down to Victoria to meet Pat Allan. We found the Montrose Apartments on Blanshard without difficulty. The building was of red brick, neither pretentious, nor squalid, but as we toiled up a long flight of stairs to the third floor, we were both most curious to see what sort of person would welcome us.

Quick steps approached, the door after I had pressed the bell, and there on the threshold stood Pat Allan to greet us. She was small and slight and fragile. Beautiful? No. Pretty? Perhaps, in an elfin sort of way, but the overall impression was one of vitality, of eagerness, of breathless enthusiasm. Mother could detect certain resemblances to Mrs. Allan, the large aquiline nose, dark hair and pale complexion. Despite the interval of many years, there was no restraint nor awkwardness, and Pat chatted away without effort. She spoke of her life in Shanghai, of the affection and generosity of the aunt who had done so much. Her sister, Dane, was happily married, and also lived in Shanghai. Pat's life had been interesting; her cultured voice, her poise and a certain charm were proof that the influence of her aunt and her schooling had been beyond reproach. She had prepared a delicious supper for us, after which it was arranged that she and Mother should have their chat together, while I paid a visit to my brother. Later, I returned to the Montrose Apartments, and by way of entertainment, it was suggested that we should attend a showing of a recent filming of the ballet, "Gaité Parisienne". At this time, the magic of color film and three-dimensional photography were somewhat primitive, and certainly by present standards, "Gaité Parisienne" would be considered a total failure. But the gay, lilting Offenbach music was delightful, and Pat's vivacious and vivid personality were in themselves memorable. Later, we drove her back to the apartment, shared coffee with her, and at a latish hour began the long drive back to the Lake.

My mother was perhaps a trifle reluctant to divulge all the details of her conversation with Pat, but implied that seldom had she found it more difficult to reach a hasty decision. For almost as soon as I had left the dinner table, the girl had locked the door behind me, closed the windows carefully, and then began, impulsively, "Mrs. Green, I can't tell you how much I have wanted to meet you, because you are the *only* person who can tell me the truth about my mother. Even when I was a child in England, she was never mentioned, and whenever I asked about her, people always said, 'Ssh, ssh, we don't speak about her', or else they would change the subject. I know there was something odd, or strange, or wrong about my mother, and I must know, I have to know! Years ago perhaps it didn't matter so much, but now it matters to me desperately, because I am engaged to marry a man in Shanghai. I want to marry him, I want to have children, but I must know the truth about my mother first. That is partly the reason why I came to Victoria. Of course it is a help for me to have Jack and his wife living near me, but I want to be independent, I don't want to feel that they must help me, or be responsible for me in any way. But until I learn something more about my mother, and her life here, I am in torment!"

I do not know exactly what mother revealed about Mrs. Allan, but I know that she must have felt that she had no right to destroy Pat's faith and hope by telling all the sordid details. How could she repeat the confession that ended with "I am what I am, rotten all the way through!" Whatever may have been revealed, or left unsaid, I feel sure that Pat was cheered and encouraged by our visit. Later, as we drove home to Greendale, there was much food for thought. How strange that the wheel of fate or destiny had brought this eager, vivacious girl back to Victoria, in her desperate quest for identity, for the knowledge that she might be free to follow the security offered by love and marriage, free from the taint that had destroyed her mother's life.

Yes, we did see her again, some months later, when she came to Cowichan to spend a long weekend at Greendale. She seemed happier, less tense and nervous. We took her for several short drives about the area; she visited The Shack, where she met Mr. and Mrs. Lomas, who must have been consumed with curiosity to see once again the person they remembered as a pathetic and neglected child. She left us a copy of a book that she had written while in Shanghai. It is entitled *"Shanghai Picture Verse,"* and bears the author's autograph. It consists of 24 short verses, on various local topics, cleverly illustrated with black and white sketches, and is dedicated to "The Shanghai Child of Yesterday and Today".

SHANGHAI BY NIGHT

Shanghai's ugly during the day,
But you should see it at night,
When everyone's jolly
And hurrying home
And all the shops are alight.
It's most exciting, and Nanking Road
Is bright as a Christmas tree;
I really don't know where to look,
There are SO many things to see:
The rickshaws and cars and jostling crowds,
And the funny things they do;
And the lights coming on
And then going out.
Oh, I LOVE Shanghai, don't you?

We did not see Pat Allan again but perhaps a year and a half later a letter arrived from Montreal. She was on her way back to Shanghai, with her husband, the wedding having taken place a week earlier. She was ecstatically happy. Someday they would return to Vancouver Island for a holiday, and would come to Cowichan Lake to visit us. This was more than 25 years ago, and we have heard nothing since.

And so, Hildegard, this is the end of the story. You will see how it could not possibly have been told by word of mouth; how bored you would have been! It may have bored you to read it, for

I have not been too skillful in my efforts to recount the details. But at least you know the story that lies behind the old stove. Perhaps I have been unfair in failing to disguise certain names, but except for Jack, Kae, and Pat, the others I have mentioned have all vanished from the scene. The Shack still stands, altered beyond all recognition. The stove is still in daily use, but what will be its final end? Many, however, are the memories that remain.

Clair de Lune
(For Pat, who may not have forgotten.)

Never before, in the history of the world, has the moon played a more important role. In recent days, millions of people, from every quarter of the globe, their skins of every conceivable hue, have goggled in awe at their TV screens, or else have gazed at the headlines and blurred scenes that have appeared in the press. But for that matter, for centuries, for thousands of years, the moon has been venerated and deified far more than all the rest of the heavenly bodies. For every ode, or hymn of joy to the sun, at least a score must have been inspired by the moon.

For those in doubt, allow me to submit a few examples. Let us begin with the realm of poetry, and offer, first of all, some random phrases from the vast legacy left to us by the Bard.

"How sweet the moonlight sleeps upon these banks."
(The Merchant of Venice.)

"O, swear not by the Moon, th' inconstant Moon,
The Moon that is caprice itself."
(Romeo and Juliet.)

"And then the Moon, like to a silver bow new
bent in heaven, shall behold the night."
(A Midsummer Night's Dream.)

"You would lift the Moon out of her sphere,
if she would continue in it five weeks without changing."
(The Tempest)

And now, other offerings come thick and fast:

"The Moon was a ghostly galleon tossed upon cloudy seas."
(Noyes.)

"Ah, Moon of my delight, that knows no wane."
(Fitzgerald.)

"And hang them up in silver icicles,
quietly shining to the quiet Moon."
(Coleridge.)

"Deep on the convent roof,
the snows are sparkling to the Moon."
(Tennyson.)

And now, let us turn to the equally vast heritage of music.

Beethoven's "Sonata Op. 27, No. 2, (Sonata Quasi Una Fantasia)" was not, we now learn, composed for the blind girl at Bonn while moonlight streamed in at the small window, but the world continues to know it as the beloved "Moonlight Sonata."

There is Debussy's "Clair de Lune," from which I have borrowed my title for this effort. Gilbert and Sullivan's operettas contain at least two references: "That placid Dame, the Moon's celestial Highness" is in *The Mikado* and "Pale Moon, to thee I sing, bright regent of the heavens" is from *Pinafore*.

In the more specialized world of grand opera, there are, I am sure, many references, but at the moment I cannot recall any particular arias, choruses, or recitatives that directly involve the moon. Of cheap lyrics and schmaltzy ballads, however, the list is endless.

Hereafter, there follows a narrative dealing with a simple and uncomplicated country woman of my acquaintance, not the least of the handmaidens of the Lord, who was able to recognize beauty in the common, and to express her admiration and reverence in an immortal phrase.

But to capture the *"mise en scene"*, one must return to a forgotten era: the Cowichan Valley as I remember it in the fall of 1933.

It had been a glorious autumn, and the promise of a bountiful harvest lay upon the land. At Greendale, as elsewhere, apples and plums fairly cascaded from the ancient trees; my father's vegetable garden was stocked to overflowing with abundance. The crabapple tree, in particular, was aglow with a glut of fruit. And herein there lay a problem; whereas pears and plums could be preserved, or rendered into jam, and apples could be readily disposed of, only a small fraction of the crabapple yield could be made into jelly.

My father, who scorned the very thought of trade and commerce, would gladly have given the crabapples away to all and sundry or fed large quantities to the cows and the old horse. But mother, who, of necessity nurtured a business-like approach, could view the situation only as a tangible asset. The crabapples must be sold, and that quickly. But to whom? A hasty rundown of possibilities followed, with disappointing results. The Boulets in all probability could not afford to buy more than ten pounds, less than a drop in the bucket. The Lomases? Well, the Lomases, despite many excellent qualities, held a hedonistic view of life in general and had no time for the pursuit of jam-making and the bottling of fruit. The Castleys had a crabapple tree of their own, the Pinsons were away on holiday; perhaps the Atkins of the Lakeside Hotel? But the Atkins were close personal friends, one could scarcely venture to ask them. The Ashburnhams? Well, one remembered the occasion when Mrs. Ashburnham had remarked wistfully, that she "wished she could learn to eat an egg that wasn't fresh." It was unlikely, then, that she would so demean herself to stand over a hot stove on a warm September day stirring a mess of crabapples. And so the list dwindled until the name of Mrs. Cassie Beech was mentioned. Why not Mrs. Beech? She was hard-working, she was thrifty, and her larder shelves groaned with home-made jam, jellies, and pickles, to say nothing of row upon row of bottled fruit. No time should be lost, then, in contacting Mrs. Cassie Beech, and closing the deal.

A word, now, about Mrs. Beech. She was a hard-working, pioneer type of woman, to whom such chores as milking cows, splitting wood, killing a chicken, shooting a deer, and similar frontier pursuits held no terrors. She was hearty, kindly, completely outgoing. Her husband, Bob, benevolent and white-haired, was employed in the logging industry in some vague capacity, as were her three sons, Harry, Dave, and Tom. Of these, Harry and Dave had married, Harry to a vivid, dark-haired girl named Ruthie (nee Schultz,) while Dave's wife was a blonde named Eva.

As a mother-in-law, I assume that Cassie possessed the necessary virtues of tolerance, patience, and tact. It had been rumored that she did not judge her daughters-in-law by the usual yardstick of domesticity and fidelity; above all things else, it was, she felt, mandatory that they should be able to swear better than a man, and in the case of Ruthie, I am certain that Mrs. Beech was not disappointed. A sister-in law, of a somewhat more elevated social level, expressed disapproval in telling those who would listen, that she had overheard young Uncle Tom, with immense patience, teaching his little nephew to "tell Cassie to go to hell." From these scattered recollections it can be seen therefore that Mrs. Beech was a woman of many parts.

And now one must wander far back through the mists of time to see the peaceful village as it was on this particular Saturday evening in early September. Such a sentimental journey suggests the device known as the "historical present".

The straggling village has enjoyed a warm hazy afternoon, the air is faintly acrid with the smoke of a distant slash-fire. A pall of fine dust has settled on the roadside fences, and on leaf and branch; the neat gardens at the Riverside Hotel and the fish hatchery are gay with dahlias, asters and phlox, which waft a faint and nostalgic essence abroad on the evening air.

"Sweet was the sound, when oft, at evening's close, up yonder hill the village murmur rose." So wrote Oliver Goldsmith, almost two centuries ago, and although the village murmur of Cowichan might not be considered sweet, it is not lacking in variety. At Hemmingsen's Field, a softball game is in progress, and the staccato crack! of ball against bat, and youthful cries of enthusiasm fall upon the ear. A feeble and sputtering whine can be traced to the Madill Chevrolet, as it totters up the gentle slope to the Riverside bridge, where it is overtaken by the Grosskleg Buick, which surges past in splendid style. Distant cowbells can be heard, tinkling in the direction of the Grant's Lake area, and the incessant yapping of several dogs obtrudes upon the ear.

And as one approaches the center of the village, the small human touches emerge. Mrs. Grosskleg is leaning across the fence, in earnest conversation with her neighbor, Mrs. Hardinge. ("Well, all I can say is, that Our Flor'nce is a *VERY* peculiar child".); Mrs. Sam Alexander (like the muezzin of old, calling the faithful to prayer) bellowing from her porch to an invisible daughter, "JOY-cee, JOY-cee;" Mrs. Reed, bouncing along the road, tennis-racket and running-shoes in hand, on her way to a mixed foursome at the Scholey's Acacia Court, and further along, beyond the railway tracks, is Nima's large black Studebaker sedan, parked beside the sinister house on the hill, its cargo of bootleg liquor being transported indoors by such as Black Gus Johnson, Shorty Sockerson, and Peg-leg Pete Olsen. This, then, is the scene as I recall it, on the far distant September evening of which I write.

Back at Greendale, supper being over, Pat and I loaded the faithful Model "A" Ford with its quota of farm produce, the regular evening complement of milk bottles, several dozen eggs, some dressed chickens, one or two boxes of apples. It was becoming dusk as we drove into the village, but the clear sunset sky, far to the west, foretold yet another fine day. The various deliveries and transactions progressed smoothly; the eggs were left at Gordon's Store, the chickens presented to the housewives who had requested them, the quarts or pints of milk left in their appointed places on back porches or in coolers. And when Pat and I had returned from our long tramp to Siwash Bay, there were but few remaining commitments, other than to importune Mrs. Cassie Beech anent the Crabapple Situation.

And, then, while Pat undertook to return to the village store to leave a grocery list, I opened the gate and walked up the untidy pathway leading to the Beech abode. In response to my knock, Bob Beech, husband of Cassie, appeared, and in reply to my question, he answered "Crabapples? Well, now, I don't know. Y' better ask Cassie. She's went over to Ruthie's to visit a spell."

After having thanked him, I walked along the rough, dusty, graveled road to Ruthie's, several houses distant. By then it had become darker, and the last hues of day were ebbing far to the west. But away in the east, a miracle was taking place before my eyes; the miracle that we see many times with indifferent eyes and closed minds, for over the distant summit of Hill 60, the golden rim of a great Harvest Moon slowly emerged, and crept gradually higher, outlining the silhouette of trees on the horizon, and bathing the valley in its unearthly beauty.

I toiled up the steep steps leading to Ruthie's front door, picked my way across the cluttered porch, and knocked firmly. All was silent, so after a discreet pause, I knocked once again, loudly. Again a pause, and then, distantly, a shuffle of footsteps, certainly not the quick, alert tread of Ruthie. And there before me stood Cassie, large, hearty, and beaming with goodwill. Before I could present my case to her, she said, by way of apology, "I guess I never heard y' knock the first time 'cause me and Ruthie was a-settin' on the steps, watchin' that old moon come rolling up over that there mountain." As she delivered herself of this deathless phrase, we gazed far down the valley, to "that there old mountain", where in its effulgent glory, the moon had risen even higher. Cassie Beech, her round red face, surrounded by a brave array of extrinsic golden curls, resembling somewhat the moon itself, (when seen through an overcast of autumnal smoke), gazed in open admiration, as if to say, "Well, I couldn't 'a done it better myself."

We exchanged pleasantries, and the pros and cons of the crabapples were reviewed. In the end, Cassie Beech decided regretfully, that she "didn't have no time this year, what with Bob being so sick and all," and so I went away disappointed, but not unrewarded.

Almost 40 years have run their appointed course since this episode transpired; Bob, Cassie, Harry, and Tom, and even Ruthie herself have been swept away to "that bourne from whence no traveller returns". The Cowichan Valley has endured countless changes; the steps from which Cassie and Ruthie gazed in reverence have long since vanished. Even the moon has suffered incredible change, and the vandal hand of man has sought with unprecedented effrontery to probe its mysteries. "And nothing 'gainst time's scythe can make defence," says Shakespeare, with infinite wisdom, yet, when from year to year, I see the Harvest Moon, ascending, in all its majesty, over the shoulder of Hill 60, I am recalled instantly to a fleeting vision of Cassie and Ruthie, "a-settin' on the steps," like two comfortable hens, "watchin' that old moon come a-rollin' up over that there mountain."

For the Apparel oft Proclaims the Man

I have been wondering, idly, why it should be that in the lives of some people, there is interwoven a thread that can be traced, again and yet again, over many years: a pattern that the person in question may be quite unaware of but which nevertheless exists. By way of illustration, let me relate my personal experiences with a certain item of apparel, and perhaps the reader may examine his own career for a similar instance.

To begin with, does it not seem strange that, during my sojourn in this Vale of Tears, now hastening with dismaying speed into its sixth decade, I have bought only *one* coat? By coat, I do not refer to a working garment: an item made from oil-skin, neoprene, "Black Diamond" rubber, or impregnated canvas. I mean an overcoat, a dress coat, a topcoat. Surely, in the civilized way of life this must be a record of some sort.

Returning to my far distant childhood, I have vague but embarrassing recollections of made-over coats, given to my mother by kind and considerate relatives and friends. One coat, in particular, fashioned from white velvet, was once worn by the small daughter of a wealthy Victoria family. In retrospect, I feel that what would now be regarded as privations and soul-shattering problems were in fact quite the reverse.

Ours was a simple, perhaps a frugal childhood, but were we deprived in any way by having no car, no telephone, no so-called conveniences, by possessing the most limited of wardrobes? I think not, for whenever such events as a twice-yearly visit to Duncan, an ice-cream cone or soft drink, or a car ride occurred, the leaven thereof remained for many a day. And how strange the paradox that the jaded, restless and frustrated youth of today seem to be searching feverishly for the simple and primitive way of life with which I, through necessity, became so familiar.

In an old album of faded snapshots is one of my brother, my father and myself, flanked by two dogs, about to start for a Sunday morning stroll. There is snow on the ground; Brian and I are wearing woolen toques, mittens and gumboots. But we're resplendent in our new coats: bulky, navy-blue, double-breasted reefer coats, with scarlet linings, and embellished with gleaming brass buttons, on each of which, if I mistake not, was embossed an anchor or some similar nautical device. We were proud of these coats; they lasted for several years; and when mine became too small, I inherited my brother's, which was perhaps two sizes larger.

My next coat, known as Andrew's Coat, was also an inheritance. Andrew's parents lived in an Uplands mansion in Victoria, but had fallen upon financially evil times, and therefore were obliged to live as frugally as possible, so that the splendid house and grounds could be maintained in pristine condition to allure and ensnare a tentative purchaser. But Andrew, despite reversals of family fortune, had grown apace and so one of his coats was passed along to me. Although it was carefully and frequently pointed out to me that the garment was *good*, and was made of a truly splendid tweed, in all truth, I never really liked Andrew's Coat. For one thing, it was too long, and yet the sleeves seemed too short. It had leather-covered buttons, which my schoolmates ridiculed, and somehow the belt was not a success. And when the coat became wet, as it often did, a strange smell emerged from the sodden cloth. I had been informed that you could always identify a good tweed by the smell when it became damp, but I was not convinced.

Eventually, however, Andrew's Coat acquired an almost permanent smell, and one of a very different order from that of the Scottish Highlands, for one day, in an unguarded moment, I left it too near an overheated stove. At length, a dreadful smell of singeing and burning aroused me, and the coat was rescued, marred by a moderate-sized hole in the lower left side. The patch that was used to repair the damage was almost, but not quite, the same shade, and almost, but not quite, the same weave. At first, I contrived to conceal it, nonchalantly with my hand or school satchel but none were deceived and finally, in contemporary phrase, I could not care less.

Andrew's Coat accompanied me to Victoria when I began my three-year interval at high school. But in due course, I inherited, again, this time from my brother, a far more prepossessing sort of coat of dark blue cloth, the sort of coat that most of my companions were wearing in the late 1920s, and I became relatively inconspicuous.

I do *not* remember, at this time, gazing longingly in the shop windows of David Spencer's and W. & J. Wilson's at the latest fashions in men's apparel; perhaps I did, but the lack of fulfilment in that direction has left no trace of inner bitterness. Did I lack decent pride? Should I have been less humble and more covetous? I simply do not know.

Brian and Trevor Green lived a halcyon life at Lake Cowichan before moving on to Victoria to complete their high school education.

During my third year at high school, when Andrew's Coat had long vanished into the limbo of things forgotten, I acquired yet another topcoat, a really splendid one. It was *almost* brand new, and had belonged, very briefly, to my brother's employer, Mr. Ross, who had decided that it was not for him. I could not understand why. Brian felt, perhaps wisely, that it would not be seemly for him to wear his boss's coat to work at the office, so that I came to be the recipient. It was a mid-season sort of coat: single-breasted, and tailored very simply from a slate or bluish-grey fabric, and a delight to wear, or to carry carelessly slung over the arm. And one fine spring afternoon, as I sauntered home from school along Camosun Street wearing the splendid coat I was transported when one of the teachers (Miss Jennie McLeod) complimented me on my erect carriage, by saying that it was not often that she saw young men stand so straight, or walk so well. Could her solicitude have been due to the aura of the coat? At any rate, I walked on air all the way home, and almost leaned beyond the perpendicular for some weeks thereafter to enhance my newfound image.

Mr. Ross's coat followed me back to Cowichan, and remained a loyal companion for many years. I believe that in the end, my father, even less concerned with origins or the dictates of fashion than I have become, acquired it. Finally it became a bit of extra padding in our dog's kennel, a strange fate for a topcoat created in the fashion shops of Toronto. But by this time, the mid-1930s, I had entered upon a new phase of the country-worker's life wherein dress coats and style had little impact. With a warm Siwash sweater, a heavy shirt, and Raintest jacket, those of my generation were well-equipped for the coldest and wettest of winter weather; a long and confining overcoat would have been an encumbrance during the daily routine.

There was, in case of necessity, a dubious dark-blue coat, once owned by Cousin Norman Hughes, of Cambridge, Massachusetts. Though of unfashionable line and cut, it bore upon the inner lining a proud label: "Wm. Filene's, Boston" to testify that it, too, had once been *good*.

A few years slipped by before my next coat made its appearance in this way. On one of my mother's visits to Victoria, Cousin Sarah had remarked, in her efficient and practical way, "Oh, Louie, Will and Lillian have left for Europe, and just before leaving, Lillian asked me to dispose of some of her things. I wondered if there might be any items that you would find useful. There's a rather good coat. The coat in question was definitely *rather good*: it was tailored from a warm, soft cloth in a dark brown and fawn check. It was almost, but not quite, a Polo Coat. And there were indeed possibilities. Lillian was tall and striking in appearance and her taste in fashion and elegance was legendary. This was the era of the mannishly-tailored coats, made forever conspicuous by the glamorous Dietrich, and the incredible Garbo. And, after all, there was a close resemblance between these and the coats worn by the debonair Robert Montgomery or Douglas Fairbanks Junior.

Yes, there were distinct possibilities. So, some weeks later, the coat and I made our way to the upstairs atelier of E. Yarr, Tailor, Station Street, Duncan. Mr. Yarr was a small man, of Belgian or perhaps Flemish origin; he was painfully bent with arthritis, and his accent was thick and guttural. But he saw at once the potential of Lillian's coat, and with faultless craftsmanship, vision and expertise, and employing tape measure, stick of chalk, and many pins, he worked out The Shape of Things to Come. And, on my next trip in to Duncan I toiled up the steep stairs to Mr. Yarr for another fitting. The result was all that I could have wished for. There was an air, a nonchalance about the splendid garment, a symmetry in the newly shaped revers, the newly shortened hem, the redesigned pockets. Some hours later, in the privacy of my own room, preening before the mirror, I felt unmistakably "the leaven of fine clothes."

All that was needed to complete the miracle was the addition of a gay and fashionable Ascot scarf, a pair of suede gloves, perhaps a cane, and the Robert Montgomery image would have been complete. In fantasy I saw myself sauntering along the Via Veneto, admiring the fountains of Rome, or striding briskly along The Strand, on a cool and foggy November morning, rather than picking my way through the puddles at the corner of Craig and Station Streets in Duncan. And finally, the proof of success occurred when, at some local soiree in the village, Mrs. (Colonel) Boyd remarked that, in her opinion, the coat looked "almost Doggy".

That coat remained a faithful companion for several years. Like a finely constructed monument or some splendid public edifice it never quite became out of style. Age could not wither it, nor custom stale, because of its initial worth. Another compliment was gathered when, on one occasion, I had been wearing it on a brief visit to Lillian's in Victoria. As I slipped out of it, she remarked, "What a nice-looking coat that is, Trevor, it's very like one I used to wear at one time." Had Cousin Sarah not been present, I would have added, "Well, to tell you the truth, Lillian, it *is* the one you used to wear at one time" but I let the moment pass.

But if my coat did not appear to suffer outward change, the times in which we lived most certainly did. We were in the throes of World War Two. Life was a *crise de nerfs* for those of us who stayed at home. Daily headlines were terrifying, radio reports were nightmarish. We were urged to sympathy and compassion for, among others, the beleaguered Russians, the victims of The Siege of Stalingrad. And there was I, safe amid the sheltering Cowichan hills still intact with a roof above me, with three meals a day, and the security of a job. How *could* I go flaunting about, in my fine coat, while thousands of Russians shivered, homeless, in the icy blasts of the merciless Slavonic winter? And so, when the first of several clothing drives for the Russians was instigated, I parted forever with my coat. It was parceled neatly into a box, and I trusted in time was to gladden the heart of some worthy and dedicated young Russian, perhaps at that very moment keeping watch from the Sparrow Hills, to help defend Moscow from attack. And I felt a touch of the nobility that comes from sacrifice and was proud in the knowledge that I was henceforth coatless, and had done my small part towards righteousness.

When I related the fate of Lillian's coat to my life-long friend Ian he was much amused, and seemed to think it hilarious that I should shiver in the fast-approaching Cowichan winter frosts while some lumpish peasant should lurch about in the Pripet Marshes, warmly clad in my coat. I did not think it in the least amusing; I still clung, though more feebly, to my concept of The Rewards of Sacrifice but I was not aware how swift would be my reward.

Soon after this, the winter days came in earnest: cold drenching rains, with a promise of snow. And one dreary Saturday evening, as I drove in to Duncan on my way to Victoria, I allowed myself to listen to the voice of reason. It was, as I have implied, a dismal night. I was cold; hands, feet, neck and shoulders were cold. *How* could it benefit anyone, least of all the Russians, for me to shiver? So, yielding to impulse, I marched myself into the Men's Clothing Department of the Cowichan Merchants, and emerged soon after with a modest but decent and acceptable overcoat of russet brown herringbone tweed. A genuine Harris tweed smelling of the heather? Not so, but a decent replica thereof, a coat of which no one need feel ashamed, a coat that would last, yet to be honest, a coat far removed from the wardrobes of Robert Montgomery, Charles Farrel, or Douglas Fairbanks Junior.

Several days later, I received in the mail a large, rather bulky parcel, and a letter addressed in the familiar handwriting of Ian's mother. With consummate tact and generosity and marked with humor, she wrote that she had heard from Ian of my offering to the cause of the Russians. She had spoken to her young nephew, Derek, who, she knew, possessed several coats that he seldom had occasion to wear. Would I, therefore, accept this coat as a small gift, in recognition of my exemplary gesture?

I removed the garment from its tissue paper wrappings and held it up for inspection. This was a coat with a flair, but a flair of another era. It was dark blue, it had a narrow, form-fitting waist and a black velour collar. It was the sort of coat to be worn under a slouch hat by a George Raft, or an Al Capone; but it held no allure for me. It was just another coat for which I had no need. The thought, of course, is what always counts so a letter of gratitude was hastily penned to my benefactress. Then, a day or so later, another pasteboard box was found, the coat neatly folded and placed therein, and another item was added to the Second Clothing Drive for the Russians. Who, I wonder, may have been the inheritor of Derek's Coat? Some portly office worker, perhaps, his wife killed or maimed, his children missing, his apartment a shambles following a murderous blitzkrieg or some young dandy, eager to impress, peeling off the navy-blue form-fitting coat, to engage in a strenuous Russian *trepak* before an admiring audience? Who can possibly say? Who may possibly know?

The events and details I have recounted occurred almost 25 years ago. There has been, due to the phenomenally mild weather this winter, not a single occasion when I required my rust-colored herringbone tweed coat. The other day, I looked at it closely as it hangs in the hall closet. It no longer looks smart; on the lower left side is a faintly discernible tracery of moth damage.

Is it, perhaps time that I should have another coat? And who, among my anonymous brethren, is at this moment reviewing his wardrobe, thinking to replace an outmoded item?

The Harmonious Blacksmith
(A Paraphrase)

"*U*nder the spreading chestnut tree the village smithy stands."

Thus begins the celebrated work of the great poet Longfellow, whose sentiments, though charming and nostalgic, are yet a far cry from the realities of the village smithy as I knew it. The nearest chestnut tree grew about half-a-mile from George's premises; no self-respecting chestnut would have ventured to take root any closer. Instead, his "shop" was protected by a large willow-tree, and by several slatternly cedars that fawned against the stained and dingy walls.

Viewed from without, the entire building was squalid in the extreme; to the left was George's abode, a dilapidated cabin where the one small window had little effect upon the darkness and gloom within. Behind this stood the outhouse, which defied all laws of gravity in remaining upright. Add to this a pile of sodden firewood, numerous tin cans in various degrees of corrosion, plus several mounds of rusted scrap-iron, and you have a fairly accurate picture of the village smithy.

But I have forgotten George's rustic bench, which occupied the foreground of the scene. While rustic in the most extreme sense of the word, the term bench is perhaps misleading. Originally, the bench had been the chassis of a McLaughlin-Buick touring car (vintage 1920); now, years later, stripped of top, body, bonnet, fenders, and wheels, the wreckage sagged upon the weeds and rubbish of the front lawn. On hot summer afternoons, George was often to be seen squatting on the running-board of his bench puffing at his pipe and gazing placidly out upon the world. There was but one trace of adornment to this scene and this, strange to say, was a magnificent climbing rose, which flung its wealth of colour and perfume about the creaking cabin door.

"Full many a flower is born to waste its sweetness on the desert air."

To waste? Well, perhaps, yet I have heard George remark, pointing to the wealth of blossom, "Them roses? Purty, ain't they?"

I had known him as a figure of mystery and dread, when, as a child, he had been pointed out to me in the village as "George the Blacksmith", a title which remained unaltered until his death. It was always "George the Blacksmith" or simply "Old George," but never George Wilmot, never Mr. Wilmot. To a small boy his appearance in all justice could strike fear and even terror. Short and squat, with a rolling, lurching gait, dark of skin, hoarse of voice, foul in speech, unpredictable in temper, this was George the Blacksmith. "They" said that he drank, cursed, and swore; small wonder, then, that one shunned him, one shrank from contact, one took to the ditch, if necessary to avoid passing him in the road.

This attitude of mine persisted for years, though later it became customary to accost him with a falsely hearty, "Morning, George," to which, if he felt inclined, he would respond with a grunt. But now from a more mature, detached viewpoint, I can see there is much I might have learned from him. There was, for instance, his tranquility of spirit, his complete indifference to places, people and things. He was in short a law unto himself. With deliberate, lurching gait, he would appear in the store where I worked behind the counter. With a glance of contemptuous indifference, he would dismiss the other customers, children and thrifty housewives, as beneath his notice. Sidling up to the counter, he would lean his greasy, black shirtsleeves upon the edge and growl out his needs. "Gimme a loaf a bread," or "Gimme a pound of tea," or "Gimme a chaw of tobacca." This done, George would complete the transaction by fumbling in his overalls pocket for his leather pouch, selecting a soiled and crumpled bill, then replacing the change, he'd replace the pouch.

Then he would collect his purchases, turn from the counter, shuffle slowly to the door and depart, leaving in his wake an olfactory rather than a mental impression: an effluence of stale tobacco, beer, sweat, smoke, and a blending of scents from more obscure sources. Once, I remember, a large bowl of massed lilies-of-the-valley had been placed in the window in aid of a charity. Their cold, chaste scent filled the store, overwhelming the more earthy smells of coffee, onions, coal-oil, and oranges, to mention but a few. But then George walked in, regarded the lilies with a sniff of contempt, and spread abroad his own more potent odour. I cannot doubt that the lilies suffered some humiliation.

Ration books were an insoluble puzzle to George; therefore he found refuge in his dignity. He would fumble in his pocket, produce the battered booklet, and say with a twisted grin, "Gimme what I got comin'," which proved his superiority, his acceptance of the inevitable, as opposed to the thrifty housewives, for whom the question of rationed goods provoked a tirade against the government, the system, the deity. As he grew older, his visits to the store became less frequent, but once a month he would bring in his pension cheque. And again, the laborious searching in his pockets, the careful signature in scratchy, spiky letters, the growled request, "Cash a cheque?" the fumbling of bills and silver, the odorous departure. Sometimes, to reassure himself, he would peer in at the door, and rasp out, "What's the time?" or even "What day is this?" On being informed, he would chuckle hoarsely, shake his head (as many a sage has done before him when confronted with the transcience of time) and turn away.

Like himself, his costume was unique and original. Black, grease-soaked denim overalls, soiled greyish-black "Hickory" shirt, whose decolletage revealed a blackish-grey woolen vest. This ensemble was completed by a greyish-brown woolen sweater-coat, the gift of a kindly housewife, in disposing of her husband's rejects. The sweater was several sizes too large for the recipient, and as the years wore on, it drooped in pendulous folds about his knees, its color slowly darkened; the buttons, too, disappeared one by one till all were gone. But here again George proved his ingenuity by employing two large blanket-pins, which added a decorative note. His cap was a shapeless black ruin, but served in some measure to shield his matted grey hair from the elements. Beneath it his swarthy, greasy face and grizzled moustache, his rugged nose, and crafty eyes faced the world.

He was not without humor, which expressed itself in occasional hoarse chuckles, and a rare twinkle of his black eyes. A drop of quicksilver gleaming in a bucket of coal-dust, and a twinkle in the eyes of George: these were identical.

Longfellow says of his brainchild: "The smith, a mighty man is he, with large and sinewy hands, and the muscles of his brawny arms are strong as iron bands." George, on the contrary, could not have been in any way called "mighty" and his hands, while large and shapeless, were in no way sinewy. His muscles undoubtedly were strong, though not "as iron bands". His hair was neither crisp, nor black, nor long, but was lank, grey, and tousled. "His face is like the tan", a more than usually dark shade of tan in the case of our blacksmith. In all fairness, I must concede that the brow of George was, at various times, "wet with sweat", but I shall not commit myself by terming it "honest sweat". And he was not given to "looking the whole world in the face" for the list of his creditors was, I have no doubt, considerable.

In the days of Longfellow, "the children coming home from school looked in at the open door". A charming rural scene! In the days of George Wilmot, the children kept well away from the smithy at any hour of the day; had they ventured to look in at the open door it is highly probable they would have been welcomed by his growl, "Get the hell out of here, you little bastards." The flaming forge and roaring bellows therefore did not attract a juvenile audience; adults, too, avoided the smithy whenever possible.

The bard's blacksmith discharged his religious obligations by dutifully attending church on Sundays in the company of his family. I venture to swear that during the 25-odd years of his residence in our village George never entered the church, nor so much as crossed the churchyard. He had no boys, nor daughter to lift her voice in song in the village choir, and I doubt much whether his thoughts turned often towards his wife, were she in her grave, or were she not. The tears that his hard, tough hand might have wiped from his eyes could have been caused, not by deep emotion, but only from a prolonged session in the beer parlor, which he visited frequently, in company with such kindred spirits as Grandpa Johnson, Louie Franc, or "Big Gus."

On fine winter days, George the Blacksmith would slowly make his way from the smithy across the road to the wharf, where he would carefully arrange himself on the handrail, to spend a social afternoon. Presently Big Gus would lumber across, later to be joined by "Poppa" Johnson, and the three old derelicts would exchange greetings, pleasantries and blasphemies. From their vantage point, they could see the shoppers, the queue at the post office, the buses disgorging their loads, the log-train switching in the railway yard. Life flowed past them, and they, secure in their backwater of age and tranquility, could and did regard it with contempt and indifference. As the day grew colder, the session would break up and the old boys would shuffle off homewards.

Few in our village will forget the year of the Big Flood. It is still a topic of perennial interest. Swelled by heavy rains and melting snow, the lake crept higher and higher till the railway yards and the main street were awash. Families from waterfront homes abandoned them for higher ground; rowboats plied between the stores. In the prevailing excitement George was forgotten. The turbid waters rose higher, flooding out the smithy, submerging the rustic bench, dispersing the wood pile and such of the tin cans that would float. The door of the cabin remained mysteriously closed as the waters came higher. But at length the flood subsided, the sodden ground reappeared, and life returned to normal. In due course George the Blacksmith emerged, somewhat thinner, somewhat less filthy, more blasphemous, but otherwise as usual. His version of the inundation was brusque and typical: "When I seen she was comin' up, I stays in me bed, and kep' the fire goin'; then she comes in at the door, and puts the fire out. When she comes over the side of the bed, I gets up on a shelf over the winda and stays there. Had a loaf a bread, and stays there four days. Gets kinda hungry last day, lots to drink, though (chuckle) she's a bastard!" (This solution makes me wonder upon the behaviour of Longfellow's friend under similar stress.)

I saw George for the last time about two years ago. He came into the store in his lurching fashion, growled a request for a loaf of bread and made his departure. It occurred to me then that he looked ill and miserable, the sweater coat hung in folds about his shrunken frame; there was no twinkle in his old eyes. But I felt no inkling that this would be our last meeting. Then, several days later, George created more stir in our midst than he had achieved in his 25 years of residence there. On arrival at the store one morning, I found a worthy citizen at the phone talking to the doctor. "We just found old George the Blacksmith out cold, better come quick, Doc!"

And so it was. His cabin had been closed for two days, no smoke had been seen issuing from the battered stovepipe. Neighbours had gained entrance, and found old George on the bed, "out cold". As word spread, sympathy spread: "Old George dead, eh? Poor old fella!" "George the Blacksmith gone, eh? Aw! Wonder who'll be next?" (And so on.)

And yet, in his passing, George managed a final gesture. While the village gossiped and sorrowed an excited youth rushed into the store. "Hot water, quick. Old George ain't dead yet, still breathing, got any hot-water bags? Send 'em over quick." Jugs of hot water and brandy were rushed across to the smithy. George, while not coming to, rallied sufficiently to survive the ambulance trip to the hospital, 18 miles distant. He remained in a coma throughout the afternoon and evening. But later that night, while the village was attending, en masse, a dance at the hall, the police constable brought final word that George, as he put it, had "pegged out". Again the expressions of sympathy. "Poor old guy, dead at last, eh?" and "Old George gone, eh? Too bad."

Longfellow ends his poem thus: "Something attempted, something done, has earned a night's repose!"

While George had without doubt attempted much in his 80-odd years, the evidence of his accomplishment were all too few. But there is no one who can dispute at least his right to a night's repose.

I'll Take You Home Again, Kathleen

Before I begin this sordid chronicle allow me to vindicate myself before my select reading public by stating that this is no simple narrative for kind hearts and gentle people. In order to depict my lady in her true colours no four letter words, however foul, should be deleted; no situation, be it never so promiscuous, be avoided; no blasphemy disallowed. In her realm, the underworld of Honeymoon Bay, Kathleen's reign was unquestioned. The Scribe, in order to become a true craftsman, must be true to his art. Therefore, my public, you shall have my unexpurgated version of Kathleen Simonson: Her Life and Times. Let the squeamish depart. We shall proceed.

I have no record of Kathleen's origin, her childhood, her youth, or the land that gave her birth. Details such as these she seldom mentioned. They are, moreover, irrelevant. I can write only about what I know. Therefore, from the swirling mists that veil the fields of memory the following facts emerge.

Kathleen Simonson, and her husband Arthur Daniel Simonson arrived in the peaceful village of Lake Cowichan circa 1939. The exact date is of little importance. They had accepted the position of "hired couple" in the establishment of Mr. and Mrs. March, whose large farm near Honeymoon Bay has long been a hive of industry as well as what is known, in contemporary parlance, as an historic spot.

I have no recollection of meeting Kathleen or Arthur Daniel Simonson at this time. They were part of a restless throng of wanderers, who attained ultimate prominence as worthy or unworthy citizens by having employed as a soft of stepping-stone the post at the March Farm. But after my association with the Simonsons had been well established, a comparison of detail with Mrs. March revealed certain of their singularities. Arthur Simonson was an indifferent labourer, and was further hampered by extreme deafness. In appearance he was thin, graying, unkempt, shabby, and unclean; in demeanor, truculent, morose, defiant, and servile by turns. Of the pair, Kathleen was unquestionably the more presentable and impressive. There was perhaps a touch of the Amazon in her build: a certain massiveness that could not be denied. This endowed her with what in another might have been a regal air, a complacent awareness of her amplitude, but what, in her, was merely an overblown coarseness.

Her hair, regrettably, was not her crowning glory. Sparse and faded, except when lately dyed and dressed for some festivity, it lay in limp strands upon her brow. There was a resolute confidence in the contours of her nose. Her lips, thin and compressed, concealed her dentures and were relieved from the non-descript by dull gleams of gold. There was hirsute space between upper lip and nose save when it had been exposed to the effects of some depilatory. Her chin, jutting and aggressive, likewise sprouted a shadowy growth. Her hands were thick and fat with short fleshy fingers, the nails of which were bitten down to the quick. But let it not be said that there was not, on rare occasions, a certain sort of bold handsomeness about Kathleen. So much then for her corporeal charms. Her character defies analysis. In simple terms she was truculent, unpredictable, shrewd, chaotic, aggressive, violent, and coarse. But let the tale unfold.

My friend, Mrs. March, has reported that Kathleen's status as a domestic employee ranked low because of her unreliability and shiftlessness. She complained that her mistress placed walnuts in the corners of the rooms to test her qualifications with broom and duster. There would be successive days when, pleading "migraine headaches", she would not appear for work at all. There was the strange interlude when she had gone to the village for the afternoon, was away for a week, and at last triumphantly returned via Vancouver (a somewhat roundabout route) with four roller canaries! And finally, there was the transfigured night when, after a sporadic burst of screams, yells, shrieks, and opprobrium, Arthur had streaked across the yard in night attire to the March dwelling for refuge where he reported that Kathleen, in an unprovoked passion, had snatched up the wood axe and had sworn to hack off his head for a token!

Soon after this Untenable Situation, (a phrase immortalized in the past by Wallis, Duchess of Windsor) the Simonsons departed from the employ of Mr. and Mrs. March and removed themselves, their possessions, canaries and cats, perhaps half-a-mile south and east to Honeymoon Bay central, where they took up residence in a shabby, squalid and elderly floathouse and it was there where, in due course, that I made their acquaintance.

At this time, I was employed at Gordon's General Emporium and among my duties was the pleasant outlet of driving twice weekly to Honeymoon Bay for the purpose of soliciting trade for the firm and delivering groceries to the regular customers. On each trip, I became more and more intrigued by what I saw of life in the abyss.

Long years ago, Rudyard Kipling added to his stature as author and diplomat by paying a very fine tribute to the city of Victoria, B.C. "To visualize Victoria," he wrote, "You must appreciate all that the eye admires lost in Sorrento, Hong Kong, the Isle of Wight, the Doone Valley." I could paraphrase this by writing, "To visualize Honeymoon Bay, you must take into account what the eye admires most in the Borghese Gardens, the Florida Everglades, the Valley of the Moon, and the Blue Grotto." And even this would be an understatement.

Thirty years ago, Honeymoon Bay was an idyllic retreat nestled between the Cowichan hills, where the clear green flood of Sutton Creek enters Cowichan Lake. Peaceful and lovely, a more romantic spot would, have been hard to find. But 30 years have intervened, and although the contours of shoreline and hills are unaltered, all else is changed. Roads, railways and crossings, telephone poles, powerlines, log-dumps, and pilings scar the scenery. The once limpid bay is crammed with log-booms, driftwood, and pilings. "No more the glassy brook reflects the day," wrote Oliver Goldsmith long ago. How true! Sawdust, scraps of bark and decayed vegetable matter float on the surface of the bay. Tin cans, in all stages of disintegration, gleam from beneath the water. Plump rats, replete with garbage, lurk on shore; underfed cats prowl along the gangways leading to the sagging floats. Clouds of dust stifle the wayfarer in summer as the logging trucks thunder down the road from Gordon River to dump their loads of logs in the bay. Wallows of mud and slush entrap the pedestrian in winter. This then is Honeymoon Bay at the present. And here, in the least presentable among the odd dozen floathouses that ringed the bay, Arthur Daniel and Kathleen took up residence.

I cannot recall the details of my first visit to the abode. But subsequent repeated calls have branded a wealth of detail upon my mind. One approached the tradesman's entrance by a narrow marshy path bordered by skunk cabbage and willow. Then came a heavy plank, deceptively slippery, leading up onto the "float" or "gangway" that bridged the space between floathouse and lakeshore. This was a treacherous structure of semi-buoyant cedar logs, to which heavy, ancient planks had been spiked, to form a sort of deck. The whole contraption was dangerous and insecure, and swayed alarmingly to an ominous, watery accompaniment, as it churned and slapped underfoot. At the far end of this, several spongy steps led up to what most nearly resembled a gate fashioned of hay wire, chicken wire, barbed wire, and assorted wooden slats.

Beyond this lay Nirvana, Elysium, Valhalla, the Venusberg, the Dulce Domum of Arthur and Kathleen. The house, long and narrow, was designed so that the three rooms opened one into the other. The back porch included a large wired-in area, wherein the four canaries might frolic, sing, and multiply. To the left of this, a battered door opened into the kitchen/living-room, which in turn led into the bedroom, which in turn opened into the spare bedroom. Kathleen's kitchen was small, littered, and dirty and at all times confusion appeared to reign. There was, I seem to remember, a cluttered table, a rusty, grease-encrusted stove, a slimy, stained sink, several shoddy chairs, usually heaped with newspapers, soiled rags or apparel, and a series of shelves heaped with chinaware, cutlery, pots and pans. There was nothing in the kitchen that was not unclean. A greasy dustiness seemed to pervade the air itself.

My approach to the floathouse was frequently heralded by a bevy of scrawny, multi-hued cats, who fled before me to disappear beneath the timbers and logs upon which the structure was built. Then I would struggle at the wire gate, pass by the aviary, and knock on the door.

Here follows a typical conversation:

Kathleen (in suspicious tones): "Who's that?"

Groceryman (pleasantly): "Gordon's Store, Mrs. Simonson. I have your groceries here."

Kathleen (in honeyed tones): "Why, yes, that's right, Trevie. Come right in, come right in. I was just waiting for you."

Groceryman: "I think everything's here, Mrs. Simonson. I've got your tin of coal oil out at the truck, I'll bring it right in. Here's the meat order. Altogether, it comes to $8.27. I have change for a $20 bill."

Kathleen: "Well, Trevie, I couldn't get in to cash Art's cheque, and anyway, there's that insurance to pay up. Put it on the bill this time, Trevie, put it on the bill, and I'll pay it next time; just write it down on the bill till next time. And I was going to tell you there was this couple Art and I met that time in Winnipeg. We were living in two rooms then, Trevie, in that little street off Portage Avenue, you know where I mean; not Main, that other street, two blocks away. Well, that would have been about 1923 no, let's see, now, 1924 I guess it was. Well, Art was working in this factory then, and I had just got down into the street when I seen this man coming over to me. Sit down, Trevie, sit down. I've got some coffee right here, just needs heating up, there's a cup right over there. Art'll be in for lunch soon's the whistle blows. Oh, and I hate to trouble you, Trevie, but here's the mail sack to take back to the post office, Mr. Scholey, his name is, I think. And you can tell that goddam sonofabitch at the railway station that next time they send the canary birds that way, for Chrissake to tell me quick, instead of leaving them to starve there like they done last time. Sit right down, sit down, Trevie, I've put some eggs on to poach, you can eat two. Them two last canaries I got, paid $12 for the pair of them, no, it was $13. Well, one of them turned sick. Don't know what it was, it seemed to eat all right, but the feathers turned sort of brown, and its eyes closed up. And here's these three letters, Trevie, if you put the stamps on them, I'll give you the money next time I get that insurance cheque. And, let's see, you better bring me six loaves next week, Trevie. That's right, six loaves. And the meat, I'd want six pounds of sirloin, not the thick, the thin kind. And the butter and six tins of milk, six will do for now. Just sit down, Trevie, your coffee's just about ready."

This is a fairly accurate representation of my weekly reception at the Simonson family home. At all times, the costume of Kathleen was unique. Whether assembled expressly for my benefit to allure and charm I could not tell. Usually, she was attired in what appeared to be a cast-off black satin slip, its shining surfaces long since dulled by stains of meat and drink. It could have equally well been, however, an imported evening gown, fashioned in the period of the Terrible Twenties. To all appearances, though of this there was no proof, she wore little or nothing beneath. Seldom were her massive legs encased in stockings but thrust into black gumboots or else soiled and beribboned boudoir slippers. There was, of course, the day I beheld the terrible apparition of Kathleen clad, not "from head to foot in song" as the poet has said but in her husband's winter underwear, strained to full capacity at the seams! I could not retain my composure at this spectacle, so that Kathleen, with a meretricious chuckle, remarked, "Well, Trevie, you needn't mind an old woman like me, old enough to be your grandmother. Awful cold out today, ain't it?"

And then there was the episode of the fur coat. Kathleen did possess a fur coat and once or twice I was privileged to see her wearing it. Once, I observed her, handsomely clad in rusty black, the fur coat flaring open to display a sunburst of dime store diamonds, her hair stylishly arranged beneath an emerald-green feathered toque, walking resolutely in the direction of the March Farm, carrying a shotgun. A startled householder, from whose window I beheld this revelation, remarked, "Jesus! See that dame out there with the rifle! I'm gettin' out!" We gazed in fascination as the blowsy Amazon disappeared behind a large stump.

One fine summer afternoon, Kathleen had outdone herself in exhausting the friendly services department of Gordon's Emporium. There were the several unstamped letters to mail, there was the mail sack to return with a blasphemous message to the postmaster, there was the appeal for an extra extension of credit for my employer. These commissions duly memorized, I sought to escape when Kathleen fixed me with an alluring smile and a honeyed approach. "I have a little favor to ask of you, Trevie. I want to send my fur coat in to Duncan for storage at the Sun Brite Cleaners. I'll just wrap it up for you so's it won't be no trouble, and then all you have to do is to unwrap it again and fold it up and just put it in a box, Trevie, any little box would do, and all you need to do then is to address it to the Sun Brite Cleaners in Duncan and take it over to the post office and ask that goddamned Scholey bastard to insure it for $75. I'll give you this 50-cent piece now, Trevie, just change this $10 for me, so it won't be no trouble for you, won't take no time at all!" During these instructions, she had wadded the fur coat into an untidy lump, enveloped it loosely in crumpled newspapers and tied it with a knotted shoelace. An hour later, during a slack moment in the store, I found a small cardboard box and drew the shining folds of Kathleen's fur coat from its paper wrapping. In so doing, I was somewhat surprised, though not incredulous, to see a humble moth, of small size and battered appearance, fly feebly into freedom. Having been trained from childhood to regard the Job Well Done as an essential aim in life, I spent far longer than one might suppose to entrap the moth and return it to the land of its birth. The persecuted Mr. Scholey protested when I told him Kathleen's evaluation on the coat. "$75 on that old chewed-up thing? Not worth $15," he expostulated.

And what of the Tasmanian wood warbler? Well, as the months had waxed and waned, Kathleen's canaries had increased alarmingly. The aviary and the nesting boxes were crowded to capacity but Kathleen's hunger for ornithological specimens was unfulfilled. "Trevie," she began one afternoon, "Just sit down over there, Trevie. And you could leave that orange box for me, too; it will come in useful. I've got this bird I've bought, Trevie, reasonable, too, only cost me $15 from this man lived across from me when we was in Winnipeg, an awful nice man he was, Trevie, a real gentleman, good-looking too. I seen this advertisement in the paper last week for these Tasmanian wood warblers, make a swell pet. Just wait, Trevie, just wait a minute. I'll have your tea all hot, just the way you like it. Well, Trevie, I paid the $15, and it should arrive at the railway station any day now. So you could go over there, Trevie, and find out if it's come yet. You could go over before you get back to the store, so it'll save you time. Here's this 15 cents, Trevie, and you can pay the balance, whatever it is, and then I might be able to make it right with you after I get Art's cheque next week and that way you won't need to worry over it." Several days later, I was summoned to the railway station to collect a small parcel for one Mrs. A. D. Simonson, Honeymoon Bay. After the interchange of coin, I was entrusted with a small wooden box, screened in front by fine wire. Within in a far corner huddled a tiny bedraggled object, malevolence and loathing ablaze in its immense black eyes. I shared, the front seat of the delivery truck with the Tasmanian wood warbler, but upon reaching Simonsonia I found no one in residence. I left the new arrival on the kitchen table, and we never saw each other again.

Time marched on, and by degrees various facts attained a doubtful clarity. It seemed increasingly dubious whether the

Simonson National Indebtedness to the House of Gordon would ever be entirely settled. Kathleen's excuses and sob-stories were endless. Her weekly demands on my time and patience increased. My employer's patience and tolerance were strained to the breaking point. And gradually, insidiously, Awful Stories, concerning Arthur and Kathleen and their way of life were wafted abroad. And even my innocent eyes were strained wide when, on a certain hot Saturday afternoon in June, I had knocked repeatedly on Kathleen's door and had shifted impatiently from side to side, under the heavy box of groceries. From within came a steady mumble of thick, incoherent voices. At last, with difficulty, I pushed open the sagging door and stumbled in, my entrance having no visible effect on the couple slumped across the kitchen table. Kathleen and a decayed gentleman, both far gone in drink, were mouthing and gibbering at each other and were wholly unaware of my presence. I managed a loud cough, and as Kathleen peered hazily at me, I said loudly, "Your groceries, Mrs. Simonson; it's Gordon's Store. I've brought your groceries." She looked up at me with barely a flicker of comprehension. Her face was swollen and livid, her hair greasy and awry, her eyes bloodshot. After two attempts, she managed to ask "What's your name, son?" I said shyly, "They call me Trevie." This modest confession produced no result. I explained my mission, and at last Kathleen seemed aware of a common bond. "Just leave the box, son," she mumbled. "See you next week. I'm awful sick, son; I don't feel good, at all." Revolted at such a picture of fallen womanhood, I retreated hastily.

Once, I witnessed a domestic quarrel of alarming proportions. I had arrived shortly before noon with a large box of groceries. Kathleen, in a burst of hospitality, had very nearly pushed me into a chair while a greasy hors d'oeuvre composed of lard, eggs, and toast, slowly congealed upon the stove, "Well, Trevie, your tea's all hot, sit down right here, and here's a nice egg for you just the way you like it," she began. At that moment, the door opened and Arthur Daniel, in work attire, shuffled in. Kathleen attended him with a wide smile, and honeyed words. "Come in, Art, my dear," she said. "Come in out of the cold. Your dinner's all ready." Art pushed roughly past her into the bedroom and slammed the door. Kathleen's benevolent aspect vanished at once, but she temporized and we conversed or, should I say *she* conversed normally. After a moment she raised her voice and said pleasantly, "Come on, Art, my dear, your lunch is getting all cold." There was no response from the bedroom and at once Kathleen's forbearance snapped. She thumped on the door and yelled, "Come out of there, you God damned yellow-livered bastard before I knife you!" Then she smiled upon me, "Come along now, Trevie, here's your tea. Art, you lousy rat, you get back in here." At the prospect of war to the knife, I invented an excuse for instant flight and left to an accompaniment of threats and shouts.

Finally the denouement of the Lost Pocketbook proved to be the breaking point in relations between Gordon's Emporium and the House of Simonson. The recounting of this sorry episode still recalls the hours of frustration and misery which hung so heavily upon me at that time. It all began when on a blazing Saturday in July I had returned to the truck from a brief visit with Kathleen, and discovered that my pocketbook, containing cash, cheques, ration coupons and a few personal papers, was nowhere to be found. But I couldn't be sure whether I had produced the pocketbook during my dealings with Kathleen. Therefore, I hurried back along the lakeshore to a neighboring floathouse where not 15 minutes previously I had made change for $5. The good housewife was sympathetic, concerned, and helpful, and together we searched along the gangways, peered into the murky water, and groped among the jungle of rushes, skunk cabbage and willow that bordered the trails but to no avail. Some minutes later, and with a fluttering heart, I knocked at Kathleen's door. From within came a scuffling sound, then a silence, and then a suspicious "What is it?"

"Oh Mrs. Simonson," I began, "Did you notice if I left my pocketbook behind when I was here a few minutes ago? I can't seem to find it anywhere. "Why, no, Trevie," replied Kathleen. "I never seen you with it at all. You must have lost it on the trail, Trevie. Wait a minute and I'll help you look." And with immense concern she followed me onto the trail, where we groveled amid slime and garbage as if the devil himself were in pursuit. At one point, Kathleen lumbered back to her porch, snatched up a hatchet, and slashed away at the defenceless willow bushes until they lay trampled and mutilated beside the pathway. But it was all to no purpose, and after a half hour thus spent, I returned to the truck heavy hearted.

The wallet contained $187 more or less, in cash and cheques, and a hoard of sugar, butter and meat coupons, which during the lean years of World War Two were of inestimable worth to the storekeeper. I returned to Gordon's Emporium in the depths of despair. My employer, while naturally concerned, was most understanding and sympathetic, but suggested that I return to the scene with all possible speed to search further. Thus, an hour later, I was renewing acquaintance with the trampled skunk cabbages and byways of the Bay area. Several kindly housewives and schoolchildren joined the search, and for an hour we peered, poked, pried, and scuffled without success. Later in the evening, almost ill with frustration, I returned, and crept along the well-worn pathway to Kathleen's door. The dull glow of an oil lamp shone through the dirty windows and I pictured Arthur and Kathleen, seated lovingly together, counting and recounting the bills and silver which totaled the $187. It was too dark for further search and too perilous an assignment to clamber up the wall and peep through the window. I felt certain that a direct approach would be unrewarded. Kathleen's last words to me that afternoon had been, "No need to worry, Trevie, you needn't worry at all. If I find your pocketbook, I'll just keep it here safe until you come with the groceries next week." So there was no recourse but to drive sadly home to a sleepless night and a gloomy future.

Despite advertising, widespread publicity, and repeated search, the wallet and its contents were never found, and to this day the mystery remains unsolved. In due course, the insurance carried by Gordons to cover such exigencies restored the loss in terms of cash and the Wartime Prices and Trade Board reluctantly produced an equivalent number of ration coupons. It is perhaps unfair to say that this unfortunate affair may have further sullied the Simonson reputation or to state that the shadow of suspicion lay heavily on their abode hereafter. Nevertheless, as time passed, the prestige of Kathleen and Arthur gradually waned, and finally, due in part to financial problems, I no longer called at their door to solicit their custom.

Perhaps a year elapsed, during which I had no dealings of any sort with Kathleen. Occasionally, I saw her, imposingly attired, seated in a taxi, in company with several decayed gentlemen, all in various stages of inebriation. Once, I saw her waiting in the rain for a bus, her plumed toque sodden, her fur coat a pulpy, muddied rag. But generally speaking, our paths did not cross, to my entire satisfaction.

Some months after this, I became involved with another family, whose presence created a stir even in the lowest region of the underworld of Honeymoon Bay. Even today, years after their departure, people still say, "Remember the Underhills? Jeez! Wasn't it a crime?" (Which is exactly what it was.) The Underhills might have been well adjusted to life in the London Slums, or Chicago's Skid Row, or even in the infamous Rue du Lappe in Paris. But in Honeymoon Bay they stood out like sore thumbs. The parents were pale, thin, and unclean but the children were horrifying to see. Scrawny, dirty, unkempt, and unwanted, they roamed along the trails and alleys of Honeymoon Bay like hungry rats. The efforts of the kind neighbors to feed and clothe them were of no avail; the public health nurse provided them with blankets so that the dog and cats (of which there were several) need not be used as bedcovers. But the children knew no other way of life and the parents' pleasure and solace was to be found only in the beer parlor several miles away. It was only natural that Kathleen Simonson and the Underhills should have much in common: chiefly the consumption of alcoholic beverages and the evasion of debt in which latter they were remarkably successful.

At about this period, Honeymoon Bay achieved notoriety due to the strange and mysterious disappearance of a certain decayed gentleman, who had been one of Kathleen's dubious satellites. As far as could be ascertained, he had arrived at the Bay from the logging camp at Gordon River with a substantial pay cheque in his pocket. Later in the day, he had cashed the cheque and had called, with several convivial friends, at the abode of Kathleen for a round of elbow-bending. Still later, when the speeder was due to return to Gordon River, he was nowhere to be found, although his befuddled friends swore that he had left Kathleen's in their company. Several days went by without a clue or trace of his whereabouts and at last the strong arm of the law intervened and a detailed search was made throughout Honeymoon Bay.

It so happened that at this time I had occasion to call at the pro-tem dwelling of the Underhills. I say "pro-tem" with reason, for the dilapidated floathouse in which they had lived became submerged, or partly so, during a heavy snowfall, when Mr. Underhill, instead of shoveling the roof clear had chosen to make an extended visit to the beer parlours and rathskellers of Lake Cowichan and Duncan.

The present Underhill residence had the advantage of being on dry land, but the disadvantage of no garbage disposal. Formerly, tins, bottles, and rubbish were thrown into the lake. Now, the mud and melting snow were composted with filth and refuse. The Underhills like certain carnivores carried with them their own particular scent, and, upon entering the sordid kitchen, I recognized at once the stale waft of dampness, mildew, unwashed dishes, garments, and bodies. Mrs. Underhill, cadaverously thin and pale, stood near the rusty stove, a trio of dirty children clutching at her ragged clothes, and there at the table, with an air of faded majesty, sat Kathleen, who appeared to be in a reflective mood. "Well, hello Trevie," she said with false cordiality, "I haven't seen youse for quite a while, that's for sure."

"No, Mrs. Simonson," I responded evenly.

"I guess you may have been hearing things about me, here and there, though, Trevie," continued Kathleen. Mrs. Underhill mumbled something unintelligible as I sought to temporize. But Mrs. Simonson swept along with relish, "Well, anyways, it ain't true, Trevie, what you might of heard, I mean. It ain't true, because I can tell you, sure as I'm alive, I seen him step off my porch and start up the trail. Of course, maybe he wasn't able to walk so good just then. We'd been having a party at my place, Trevie, just a little party for Art's birthday. But, Art showed him to the door, anyways, and shone the flashlight and I seen him head off into them willow bushes. But you know what they're saying, Trevie? They're saying that I shoved him off the float and into the lake! ME! How do you like that? I heard they're going to drag the bay tomorrow, but Jeez, wouldn't it be somepin fierce if they found the (here a suspicious glance at the three young Underhills, who, with snarled hair and unclean faces gazed in fascination at the narrator) "found the B-O-D-Y anywhere around my place?" I expressed sympathy and concern, and Mrs. Underhill nodded glumly over Kathleen's persecutions.

"The mills of God grind slowly, but they grind exceeding fine" is an old saying, and though in this case they may have ground even more slowly than usual, truth is stranger than fiction. When the Simonson floathouse was towed to one side, sure enough, the B-O-D-Y was revealed, and the arm of the law finally moved into action.

Nothing could be proved against the Simonsons, for of witnesses there were none, and nothing could shake Kathleen's protestations of innocence. But nevertheless, in a few days the infamous duo departed from Honeymoon Bay for Duncan to be seen no more.

Seen no more, did I say? Seen in print, once or twice over the years perhaps for the usual reason. "A.D. Simonson was convicted in court last Monday of being intoxicated in a public place and fined the sum of $25 and costs." The name Mrs. Kathleen Simonson could be equally well substituted in the above statement.

Then, one wet wintry night, Yvonne and I, pacing the midnight streets of Duncan in search of a coffee bar, noticed in the shadows of a side street a figure shuffling towards us in a sinister fashion. Although the light was poor, there was no mistaking the once rakish green feathered toque, now a sodden ruin, the dripping fur coat, shabby and threadbare, the lurching gait, the thick, shapeless ankles. The queenly confidence had fled to be replaced by an air of hostile weariness. And I? What was my initial response to such a sorry spectacle of fallen womanhood? Though I confess it with shame, I cannot dissemble. As many of my brethren have done throughout untold pages of history, I "passed by on the other side." As if in reproach, the words of an old favorite song, far too long forgotten, slipped across my mind:

> "I'll take you home again, Kathleen, to where your heart will feel no pain, and when the fields are fresh and green, I'll take you home again, Kathleen."

Brian, Trevor, and Louie Green, photographed in the early 1920s.

The Mesachie Man

*N*o anthology of Cowichan stories could be considered complete without reference to a certain creature, (mythical or otherwise, who can say?) generally spoken of as "The Mesachie Man". But it is difficult, if not impossible, to establish contact with anyone today to whom the Mesachie Man is more than a vague and tenuous fiction. Therefore my modest statements are the result of probings and delvings amid a great mass of childhood memories, some of which may well be distorted by the passing of many years. One thing is certain, however: there is no one alive today in our village who actually saw the Mesachie Man.

When my father arrived at Lake Cowichan, during the year of 1886, a totally different world and way of life existed. Where now are houses, shops, roads, playgrounds, railway tracks, schools, and churches was one vast, sombre forest, through which the river flowed on its way to tidewater. The river and the winding wagon trail to Duncan were the only means of access to what is now a thriving centre. And in the midst of this God-forsaken wilderness or earthly paradise (depending on opposing points of view) the Mesachie Man had his being.

My father always appeared to enjoy talking about this strange being, and my brother and I would listen, fascinated, to spine-chilling narrations about the blood-curdling yells that rent the night air. They were *not* the screams of a cougar, they were altogether different. And, of course, there was the dreadful evil face with beetling brows and prognathous jaw, once seen peering over a log by a pioneer friend of father.

In this enlightened and worldly age, I am not able to decide whether or not the Mesachie Man was occasionally employed as a threat or a weapon but I used to hear, "You'd better get that wood into the house before it gets too dark; it's the sort of night that the

Mesachie Man used to come around." But this is perhaps unfair to my father, and I don't believe he would have deliberately stooped to such trickeries.

My mother, who did not appear at the Lake until about 1908, was thus a mere upstart in the pioneer hierarchy, and therefore could not be expected to have seen or heard the Mesachie Man. She kept her skepticisms closely guarded however. Though she had neither seen nor heard the Evil One, she did not denounce him as being a creature of fiction nor did she devoutly believe. But Aunt Nan, she was made of sterner fibre.

Aunt Nan was my father's younger sister, and had arrived at the Lake soon after the "original" Riverside Inn was completed. In her official capacity as cook and hostess, she fulfilled her duties nobly and was much attracted to the pioneer way of life. In later years, she, too, had fascinating stories to tell of the early days.

Since, at this time, she was the only white woman at the Lake, she was an object of great interest to the few native women who spent summer months camping beside the river while the men constructed their canoes from the great cedars that grew in such abundance. Aunt Nan described how, in the late evenings, the kitchen door would creak open, and one or two native women would creep stealthily in to watch and wait. Aunt Nan would talk quietly to them and offer them food and sometimes they would touch her shoes and her clothing, obviously fascinated by this strange woman who had appeared in their midst.

But I digress from the Mesachie Man. Aunt Nan's faith and belief in him was a powerful force, in fact almost a religion and years afterward, in the epoch of the Terrible Twenties, she could become quite eloquent on the subject. "What!?" she would snort, to any doubting Thomas, "No Mesachie Man? Of course there's a Mesachie Man. I heard him, didn't I? That terrible wailing scream in the night? Certainly there's a

Mesachie Man." When closely scrutinized, Aunt Nan had to admit that she had never actually *seen* the dread figure but she was convinced that he lived in a cave on Mesachie Mountain. The native people were terrified of him, she maintained, and the women and children rarely ventured from the camp on the shore on that account. She and my father both were convinced that in the more distant forests, the Indians [sic] had constructed deep pits, skillfully covered and concealed by a thin framework of limbs and poles and artfully overlaid with moss and twigs. Into these pits they occasionally entrapped an unwary deer or perhaps a bear, but it was the Mesachie Man whom they really intended to capture.

The origin of the Mesachie Man like most early legends was obscure. My father and Aunt Nan both averred that he was half-man and half-gorilla, an alarming combination, and that he had somehow escaped from a sailing-vessel that had foundered years before on the west coast. Was he destined to become an exhibit in a zoo or a sideshow somewhere on the notorious waterfronts of Seattle or San Francisco before fate thus intervened? This we shall never know, nor shall we ever know the truth of Aunt Nan's sinister allusions to the many native women whom the monster was assumed to have dragged away to his cave to be seen no more.

When my brother and I, in our youthful innocence, would ask Aunt Nan what the Mesachie Man had *done* with the women she would say, "Well, I don't know anything about *that*, but they were Never Seen Again!"

In his book of the Cowichan Valley, entitled *Kaatza*, Mr. [Jack] Saywell writes, "According to a story told to Frank Price by Nitinat Charlie, a reasonably loquacious native of his day, there was a fierce, inhuman monster that used to roam the mountains around Kaatza. He was called a man, but had many characteristics of an animal, such as claws, hair, and the head of a bear. With many tellings, the legend grew, and the Indians became much in awe of this creature, and avoided certain parts of the Lake area, such as Mesachie Lake, possibly because the monster was supposed to have come from the west coast via the Robertson River. Indians with a flair for story-telling could always create a shiver of apprehension around a campfire by relating personal experiences with this creature."

But no one could create more shivers of apprehension than Aunt Nan, for in her shabby living-room in the old creaking house on Fernwood Road in Victoria, in the dim light of the primitive electric bulbs, she would say, as the wind wailed outside, "It was on just such a night as this that we used to hear the Mesachie Man in the early days at the Lake. We always fastened the windows inside and bolted the doors and sat in the dark, and then we would hear that terrible scream!" Again, it was of no use to remonstrate, "But Aunt Nan, couldn't it have been the wind or even a cougar?" for the fierce little woman would reply, "Of *course* it was the Mesachie Man. I *heard* him, didn't I? I was there!" To which, of course, there was no reply.

And who, after all, am I to be skeptical? Several years ago, for the first time in my life, I heard a screech owl in the unearthly hours before dawn. It was like nothing I have ever heard, before or since, and it was not until several months later that an erudite friend enlightened me. Hearing it thus for the first time alone I could well have believed in trolls, giants, spectres, and the Mesachie Man. Perhaps somewhere, in a remote fissure on Mesachie Mountain, or on Mount Cheechako, there lies a lonely cave. Perhaps somewhere in the few remaining acres of virgin forest, buried deeply beneath a carpet of moss, embroidered with ferns, there is a skeleton. In several more generations, even this legend will be laid to rest. Perhaps no greater truth is to be found than in this paraphrasing of Holy Scripture, "The fool hath said: There is no Mesachie Man."

Miss Cave

*D*uring this long, dark, and wet day, I have been idly rummaging about among distant memories and have felt that this anecdote relating to one of the many hired helps that came and went during long ago summers at Greendale might be of interest.

As the years progressed, and more visitors and fishermen patronized our small resort on the river, it became necessary, if not essential, to engage a resident cook each spring and many and varied were those who responded to the advertisements in the Victoria, and occasionally, the Vancouver papers. To review, briefly, there was Miss Winifred Austin from Quamichan, pleasant and cheerful, but physically unable to weather the long hours and days over a hot stove in a small kitchen; there was Ellen Langton, with whom I already have dealt; there was Miss Thornhill, a complaining and acid-tongued lady, who soon went on her way; there was Miss Ruby Stone (sister of a local lumber tycoon), freshly out from England, fashionably and elegantly attired, who could scarcely boil an egg let alone make porridge yet demanding that she be introduced to the guests, the male guests in particular. Then there were Ah Tem, and Wo Hip, both Chinese, the first a formidable creature, with a vicious temper, and skillful in the wielding of cleaver and carving-knife, the latter thin and scrawny and obviously ailing; there was Frances Johnson, there was Mrs. Barnett, there was Nellie Stalker: each and all of these candidates had his or her history, his or her frustrations and triumphs, but of them all the name of Miss Cave stands out distinctly.

Miss Cave had replied to the appeal that my mother had sent in to the Victoria paper ("WANTED: Capable Cook-General for small resort on Cowichan River, from mid-May to late September. Reply to Box XX, *Victoria Daily Colonist*") and to judge from her response she appeared to be eminently satisfactory. And thus, perhaps a week later my father met the noon passenger train from Duncan at the local railway station and drove Miss Cave and her few items of baggage home to Greendale.

My brother and I, each spring, were always anxious for a preview of the new incumbent, so that we might sit in judgment to predict how long the lady would last. And from the beginning we were most favorably impressed as I think were my parents but at that point none of us could foresee the future nor the destiny that decreed that Miss Cave would have left us long before the summer was over.

In appearance Miss Cave was a tall woman, large but certainly not fat. She was very pale, and her abundant black hair, parted in the middle and drawn back from her face in two dark wings made her look paler still. We found her pleasant and most capable but there was a definite reserve. Little was ever revealed concerning her background or history other than that she had lived until recently in Redlands, California where, I believe, she had worked for a family who owned a large citrus orchard. Then she had come north to Victoria, and had been companion-help to a poor woman who had lost her only son in World War One, or as it was termed then, The Great War. This woman (was her name Mrs. Bates?) refused to allow herself to accept the fact of his death and believed him to be alive and ever-present, but invisible; this attitude was not so peculiar during the aftermath of The Great War in and around Victoria. Mrs. Irving, the wife of Chief Justice Irving, believed that her son, Beaufin, slain on the Western Front, was alive and well, and at any moment might arrive home; therefore, a special chair was kept for him, which no one else might use, and his meals were served as usual in the dining-room. Through this self-deception, ridiculous and pathetic as it might seem in retrospect, such survivors as Mrs. Bates and Mrs. Irving, could make their lives endurable for their few remaining years.

Miss Cave soon fitted admirably in to the busy daily routine at Greendale. She was always up and about early to prepare a breakfast for brother Brian and me in the small kitchen and later a more formal breakfast for the guests in the dining room or outdoors on the verandah, depending on the weather. Then there was the lunch to prepare and stacks of dishes to be washed and dried between meals. This is not to say that my parents did not assist for they most certainly did, as did I in later years. But on scorching July days, the little kitchen with its wood-burning range became an inferno and there were times when our poor Cook-General appeared white and exhausted.

Trevor, left, friend Billy, and Brian grin at the camera from the dock on the river.

It was perhaps for this reason that each evening after work, when the kitchen was restored to order and slowly beginning to cool off that Miss Cave would retire to her tent, pitched beneath the cedar trees near the driveway, and later emerge, in bathing-suit, bathing-shoes and wrapper, and make her way down to the swimming-pool, a hive of activity during the day but generally deserted by evening. There she would slip off her wrapper, step off the float, and take several leisurely strokes in the shallow water, enjoying the refreshing effect, before returning to her tent, a few minutes later. Her candle might burn dimly for another hour or so but then it would be extinguished and we would not see Miss Cave again until the following morning. This pattern was well established by mid-summer, and those who met her even briefly were impressed by her manner and appearance in addition to her considerable skill as a cook.

And so, on a delightful evening in early August 1922, Miss Cave made her way as usual down to the river for a refreshing interlude after what must have been a hot and harassing afternoon of preparation since perhaps 20 visitors would assemble at 6 o'clock for dinner on the verandah. Upon reaching the float, she removed her wrapper and prepared to step down into the water.

Meanwhile, the Citizens of Tomorrow were enjoying themselves in their own fashion. There were the three Lawson boys, Ian Ross, Sandro Bullock-Webster, Rocke Robertson, his elder brothers, Bruce and Allan, their sister, Marian, my cousin, Mary Swinerton, my brother, and myself. There was usually a noisy game of baseball in progress but Run Sheep Run, Hide and Seek, and Throw the Stick were equally popular. Another fascinating diversion, accompanied by screams and frantic scurrying about from the young girls, was to watch the bats swooping low in the woods near the creek. (For some reason, one seldom ever sees even one bat nowadays!) Every girl, rich or poor, fat or thin, dark or fair, firmly believed that a fate worse than death was as nothing to the perils of having a bat entangled in her hair, but I have yet to meet the girl or woman who ever suffered this indignity.

Then as the long twilight lengthened into dusk the word came, vaguely, that there was someone in the river and that none of us were to investigate, nor were we to go near the main house. Rumour and conjecture flew about wildly but at last, someone, (was it Dollie Bullock-Webster or Helen Robertson?) informed us of the facts: that Miss Cave had been found lying at the bottom of the river, and that Mr. Lawson and Mr. Ross and my father had managed to pull her out, and no one knew if she were alive or dead. Meanwhile, we were all to be as quiet as possible, *we* were not to go *near* the house; we would, in all likelihood have to put ourselves to bed, and if we could all gather together and pray for Miss Cave to live, it *might* help!

Fifty-seven years have passed since that memorable night, and now I cannot be too certain of details. We knew that somehow Miss Cave had been brought up to the main house, (how? was she carried? was she lifted onto a stretcher?), that a roaring fire had been kindled in the fireplace, that artificial respiration was being applied, but none of us went near the house. I do not think that any of us, the children, spent a sleepless night; by 10 o'clock we were too tired, physically, from the day's activities of swimming and games, and of hiking in the woods in search of wild berries to lie tossing and turning, worrying over the fate of poor Miss Cave.

But next morning, there was rejoicing throughout the camp. Miss Cave was alive and had come around several hours after she had been dragged out of the river. And now she was sleeping, and we must *all* be very quiet for the next two days. While the others were ministering to the still remote form on the floor in front of the fireplace, my mother had hurried to the village on foot to telephone from the Riverside Inn for a Duncan doctor. But when she had reached the Riverside, a sort of miracle occurred, for not only was there a doctor (on holiday) registered there, but a nurse as well. (The doctor, incidentally, was to have returned to Vancouver the next day!) And so the doctor drove Mother and the nurse back to the scene of activity where the others, meanwhile, were doing all in their power to restore life to the unresponsive body. While the men, Harry Ross, Harry Lawson, and my father, took turns at applying respiration, the women, Jennie Ross, Dollie Bullock-Webster, and Mary Lawson, heated water on the kitchen range and applied hot cloths to the chilled body in an effort to restore circulation. (A large pot of soup stock that had been steaming all day on the stove was also used for this purpose.)

Trevor Green, author of this book, relaxes in a chair at Greendale.

When the doctor arrived on the strange scene, dimly lighted by the kerosene lamps of that epoch, he authorized a more practical and up-to-date method of respiration (could it have been the Shafer method?) and for another hour, the dedicated labour continued. Then, at last, (as reported by my mother) the faintest quiver or shudder passed over the inert body bringing hope and rejoicing to those who had laboured for so long. And as the respiration was continued, more rhythmically now, there were further faint quiverings and at last, a long hesitating sigh. And perhaps an hour later, normal breathing had been established, and the faintest tinge of color returned to the ashen face, while the hot cloths were re-applied as seemed necessary.

At last, around dawn, Miss Cave was carried into the small bedroom leading from the verandah, the nurse was provided with a cot, and the rest of the group straggled off to catch a few hours of much-needed rest. And all that day and much of the next a strange air of quiet prevailed. There were no noisy games, no wild shouts from the river at swimming time. We all were sobered, to say the least, by the near tragedy. Mother and Dad managed to cope with the cooking and the serving of the meals, and most of the guests nobly helped out in the kitchen and in dealing with the mounds of dishes heaped about the sink and drain board.

Reports of the condition of Miss Cave were vague; she slept a great deal, and when awake could scarcely speak for in her earlier state of panic, or perhaps a sort of premature phase of rigor mortis, she had bitten her tongue very nearly apart, and until hours later when the muscles relaxed completely, no human force could separate her jaws.

Several days later, when she was able to speak coherently, in reply to earnest questioning she said that she could remember distinctly walking down to the float, and kneeling down to adjust her bathing shoes before stepping into the water. She had no recollection of taking her slow and careful strokes but remembered clearly and distinctly walking back from the river, past the hayfield, and on to her tent, where her candle still burned! This statement I find extraordinary; it was as if she had been spared the horror and fear of death by drowning but had passed through her ordeal unharmed to return to her small canvas haven, to be restored by sleep for the routine of the next day. How strange!

But here is the report from Mr. Lawson and from Mr. Ross, who had been fishing that evening one upstream one downstream from the swimming pool. For no apparent reason, Harry Ross had ceased his fishing for the evening and returned upstream and in passing the pool had seen Miss Cave's wrapper and one of her shoes at the edge of the float, and dimly visible, in the deep water, a form lying on the river bottom. He shouted for Harry Lawson, who came with all possible speed, calling for help as he did so, and the two men, aided by my father, who had heard the shouts, managed to pry the heavy body into shallower water. (I say pry because in the deepest part of the pool, and in the rapidly approaching dusk, it was impossible to rescue Miss Cave by diving in to reach her. Fortunately, the old dugout canoe that served as transportation across the river was half-filled with water, and therefore remained in position, while the two men pried and pushed with long poles until the body could be lifted out of the water and later be taken to the house.)

The version of the Vancouver doctor was that, unknown to Miss Cave, she was afflicted with what he termed "a goitre heart", a term with which we were not familiar. The heat of the day, the stifling kitchen, had proved too much for the weary body and, as she knelt at the edge of the float, Miss Cave had fainted and had pitched forward into the cold water.

The rest I have reconstructed as well as I can remember.

A week later, on the advice of the doctor, Miss Cave was well enough to leave us and return to Victoria, where she was to spend at least a month in quiet surroundings before thinking of seeking further employment. We were all touched by her gentle humility and by her deep concern for having caused so much trouble to everyone involved. And she said to my mother, "You know, you should have let me go. It would have been so easy and now I'll have to face it all again someday."

She kept in touch with us for several months. Her last letters, I believe, came to us from Redlands, California, by which time she seemed to be in good health again. But years afterwards, we still wondered about Miss Cave, about what her past life might have been, her present, and her future.

Old Tom

*W*hen we called him "Old Tom", it was not necessarily a term of contempt. He would of course have been deeply honored if we had addressed him as "Mr. Marley" (as the occasional deferential customer sometimes did,) but even "Old Tom" sounded better than "that bloody old fool", or "that crazy old bastard", or similar epithets from his detractors. I had the privilege, if such it can be termed, to work with Old Tom for several years, in the far-off days of Gordon's Emporium and although I cannot honestly regard him as The Most Unforgettable Character I Have Ever Met nevertheless he created over the years a truly indelible impression.

Early memories of Old Tom are regrettably vague; but I remember that as a result of shell-shock in World War One he would disappear from the scene occasionally to vanish behind the protective walls of "Essondale" [the provincial mental hospital], while his wife and three children managed as best they could. Perhaps it was because of this affliction that I was, as a young lad, a little frightened of Mr. Marley and kept my distance when I saw him approaching. For there was at times a strange glitter in his steely grey eyes and once in a while we heard of how Old Tom (who was then not so old) would dive beneath the bed, or squeeze himself into a closet, convinced that at any moment a bomb would fall.

We heard that on one occasion when Mrs. Marley had a number of friends gathered about the tea-table, without warning the door crashed open, and Tom fell into the room, shouting, almost bellowing, "'Urry, 'urry! Run fer yer lives. The Germans is coming, the 'ole bloody lot of 'em. Get the 'ell out quick while there's still time enough!" (One can only imagine the consternation that ensued!) Loud explosions and sudden gunshots or the backfiring of internal combustion engines could strike similar terror and frenzy in the mind and brain of Tom, so perhaps there may have been some excuse for the trepidation that I, and others of my schoolmates sometimes experienced.

But when Mr. Marley returned to the Lake from treatment, he would return peaceably to his jobs, for sometimes he worked on the roads ("fer the gov'mint"), or cut vast amounts of cordwood for the cookhouse at the nearby logging camp, or at times he would function as general handyman, mowing the occasional lawn, perhaps painting a house, or mending a roof. His wife was an exemplary woman, most of her working hours devoted to bringing up the three children (two sons, Tom and Ed, and daughter Ellen.) Mrs. Marley's house was spotless, her garden a model of industry, her children neat, polite and hardworking. But she did not emerge as quite such a forceful, unbridled character as her husband; she did not rebel as did he against much that most mundane souls would meekly accept.

156

There was, I remember, a hiatus of several years when it was believed that Mr. Marley would never return from the confines of the asylum; he was reported to be "vi'lent"; references to "solitary confinement" and "straightjackets" were made from time to time and sympathetic though reticent concern was felt for the family. But Ed and Young Tom proved their worth by working hard at various jobs, young Ellen delivered newspapers, and Old Tom's war pension helped to ease the financial stresses.

And in due course, word was passed around that "Old Tom Marley's back home again, out of Essondale for good; wonder what he'll do now?"

For by now he was definitely old and had been swept aside from the mainstream of activity in the village to the quiet backwater of old age. What was there that he could do? Well, he could work and often did for Mr. Gordon cutting the lawn, tending the graveled drive, digging out and burning stumps, perhaps even washing Mrs. Gordon's Studebaker. Thus the weeks and months passed by.

Then one evening my employer remarked, "I'm thinking of giving Old Tom Marley a chance in the store, he's supposed to be quite all right now, there's lots of little jobs he can do around here, he's a good worker, not a lazy bone in his body. We'll try him for a few months, and see how it works out."

And so Old Tom came to work at Gordon's Emporium, remained for several years, and I am sure was convinced that but for him the business would have lapsed into bankruptcy before many months had passed. At first, we treated each other with exaggerated politeness; he was Mr. Marley, I was Mr. Green, but before long, a more informal attitude prevailed, when it was hinted "Why'nt ya call me Tom, same as hevery-body else?" This, after all, was logical, and to him I became Trivver, and continued as such to the end of our association. To begin with Tom held back. We were often informed that, "I knows me place, and I keeps to it." But as the months slipped away a lofty arrogance could be traced and when employed to excess, could drive us all past the point of exasperation.

Tom's duties at first were menial, it is true. He was supposed to help with the daily sweeping, empty the garbage, assist in filling the shelves, carry grocery boxes out to the cars in the parking lot, wash the windows on occasion, help with the deliveries, and make himself useful in other ways. But he had his limitations as well; he was not entrusted to collect the mail each morning, nor to answer the telephone since his handwriting only he could decipher, and at no time was he permitted to touch the cash register. This meant that provided Old Tom remained within his confines, so to speak, all should go smoothly and for the most part it did. For he did work hard and there were seldom times when he stood about hands in pockets, which was more than could be said for some of the more youthful incumbents, fresh from school, who believed (or were led to believe) that the only way to struggle up the ladder to success was to begin with an apprenticeship of sorts in the House of Gordon.

In appearance, Tom was not to be readily overlooked. Though not above average height, he could be best described as burly. His face, possibly finely chiseled during the far-off days of his youth, was stern and rugged. Beneath bushy brows, his piercing grey eyes surveyed the world critically and uncompromisingly.

When, at times he would fish out his glasses (thick lenses with heavy black rims) from his pocket and adjust them on his rugged nose, the grey eyes, magnified tenfold, seemed as relentless as probing searchlights.

His hair, seldom other than neatly brushed, was silvery white, and was perhaps his most arresting feature. I can see him now, as I write, busy with his broom, emptying a sack of potatoes, opening a crate of oranges, loading a sack of cow feed into a customer's truck. I can see the fierce determination, the grim disapproval of his customary expression; I can hear him say gruffly to one of the staff, who had carefully swept a section of the tiled floor, "'ere,

Sanford, lets 'ave yer broom, I'll show ya 'ow it's done," and I can see Mrs. Sanford swallowing her wrath and flouncing away in the opposite direction.

For the first year or two of his employment our paths did not often cross; that is to say we did not function as a team, but later, with a reshuffle of staff, I found myself often driving the delivery truck of an afternoon with Old Tom as my helper. When someone might ask Tom if he could drive, he was always prompt with his answer. "Me drive? No, Sir! If I 'ad a car, I'd be out drivin' all over the place, wouldn't stay 'ome at all; that wouldn't be no good. No, Sir, ya won't catch ME drivin'."

His talent for self-justification was truly exemplary. Later, as I knew him better, it became obvious that the forbearing Mrs. Marley made frequent and extended visits to Vancouver in order to retain her sanity and tolerance. We would be told, "The Missus 'as went to Vancouver for a while, stayin' with Ellen, so guess I'll be batchin' fer a few weeks," or he would say, "Wife's comin' 'ome t'morra, been stayin' with Ellen fer a while. 'Ere, Trivver, 'ere's me grocery list, ya can write it up. No 'urry, just take yer time." And once, in a rare burst of confidence, he said, "Some of them busybodies around 'ere's been 'intin that me and the Missus ain't gettin' along so good. Well, Trivver, it's like this. She likes ter go over and stay with Ellen and the kids an' I likes ter stay 'ome. What I says is, one of us 'as ter go first, and t'other's goin' ter be left alone, so might 's well git used ter it before 'and, seems ter me."

Several afternoons each week, Tom and I would start out on the delivery run. Our various customers were divided, geographically into three areas: South, Hundred Houses, and North, and it was a tacit understanding that we should, always "go South" first. Therefore, around half-past two, Old Tom would approach me, and say, not unreasonably, "Well, I'm ready ter go South, Trivver, soon as you are," or with a hint of reproach, "It's arter two o' clock, Trivver, 'ow about startin' South?" and we would pile into the old grey Dodge, the groceries heaped in more or less orderly fashion, behind. At times, Tom would be silent, his craggy features compressed into grim lines of disapproval.

As we went south stopping here and there en route, a mutual agreement had developed between us that he would deliver the groceries to houses on the right side of the road and I would deal with the deliveries on the left side.

We would stop accordingly, and Old Tom would clamber stiffly out, go around to the back of the truck, and carry the box to the back door of the house in question. His method of approach never varied; there was no discreet knock at the door, no false cordiality, no cheery "Good afternoon, your friendly delivery man from Gordon's."

Instead, he would thump on the door, or push it open roughly, lumber across to the nearest table, and dump the contents of the box out in a confused heap, his conversation limited to "'Ere's yer groceries", or "'Owdy, mum, fine day."

But on rare occasions he would unbend and a frosty humor could be discerned. Once, (and I relive my embarrassment) he and I, each with a large box of groceries, had reached the abode of Mrs. Beer Singh, whose husband worked in a nearby sawmill. She was short and rounded; she dressed in long flowing robes, and was usually heavily veiled; she spoke no English, but a reserved smile and a gracious nod were all that seemed necessary.

On this particular day, Tom burst open the door to reveal Mrs. Singh, leaning over her washtub, vigorously rubbing garments upon a washboard.

Instead of the usual expostulations and apologies that would have been in order in other homes, the lady favored us with a mild glance from her beautiful eyes, and resumed her labours.

But Tom in an effort to be pleasant and humorous, having pushed the grocery-box onto a nearby chair, next proceeded to give Mrs. Singh a tremendous dig in the ribs, at the same time remarking roguishly, "That's right, Mum, washee clothes, washee clothes, make 'em clean!"

I felt compassion and admiration for poor Mrs. Singh, who gazed upon Tom with womanly dignity and continued to scrub at her clothes.

But when we were safely back in the Dodge and I debated within myself whether or not I should remonstrate with Tom, he remarked with much complacency, "That's the way to treat the women, Trivver; you got to kid 'em along; that's what they likes, just keep kiddin' 'em along." And these pearls of wisdom from one far advanced in years swept away any suggestions I might have made concerning a "respectful attitude towards the customer".

Sometimes, often, in fact, when we had "gone North" and were returning to the Emporium along the straggling village street, Old Tom would suddenly and announce "Stop 'ere," and we would come to a halt before the Lake Cafe.

Here we would descend and cross over to the entrance and Tom would thrust open the door, stride majestically in and announce in a lordly way, "Trivver and me wants a cuppa coffee, better 'urry up there, 'n don't keep us waitin'," whereupon the waitress would scurry about obediently, and Tom might converse with adjacent customers.

"'Owdy, Jim. 'Ow's the Missus? 'Ow come I never see you at Bingo no more? You'd oughta come out and bring the wife, do 'er good." Or, "'Ullo there, Joe, 'ow ya doin' there, boy? Y'ain't lookin' so good. 'Ad the 'flu, eh? Well, I 'ad it meself a week back. Guess we're none of us gettin' no younger, Joe, and that's 'ow it goes."

And when we had finished our coffee Tom, with imperious dignity, would slap the coins down on the counter, and we would depart.

Often our passage through the village streets evoked pertinent comments from my assistant.

"There's old Ken Gillespie over there, 'oldin up good fer 'is age too, ain't 'e, been 'ere 's long as I kin remember." Or, "'Oo's that 'oman comin' out of the drug store, Trivver? Mrs. Lincoln, eh?" (A prolonged sniff of disapproval and then a succinct comment of two words) "'Air's dyed!"

Or, "This 'ere road's a disgrace, I tell ya. Never seen it so bad, with all them pot 'oles. It's a wonder they wouldn't git around to fixin' it." Or, "Better slow down 'ere, Trivver, ya never know what them kids is goin' to do when school's out; ya better let that train get over the crossing before ya goes a'ead."

There were times, it is true, when I seethed with revolt under Old Tom's domination but I felt that it would have been beneath my dignity to explode in righteous wrath and say, "Oh, shut up, you bloody old fool, and mind your own business." Tom would have been shocked and offended, of course, and I would have been ill with recrimination by the end of the day. So I chose to regard him in his most annoying phase as a sort of major thorn in the flesh, a tribulation that one must somehow endure. I felt, too, that if I could surmount the vexations so imposed the lesser ones would scarcely exist. So I permitted myself to be humiliated, frustrated, and embarrassed without, I trust, revealing at any time my inner attitude.

After one especially trying afternoon, when I had been cautioned about the hazards of school children, parked cars, trains, running short of gas, how, when and where to stop, and at what pace to proceed, I was almost ready to burst with rage and irritation, and I struggled to contain my wrath. Tom, sensing perhaps despondency in my monosyllables, sought to cheer me up by saying as we returned to the haven of the Emporium, "Ya know, Trivver, you're gettin' more like me hevery day, always tryin' to 'elp people." I could only think blindly that if I were indeed becoming more like Tom every day, then how apt the words, "Come, sweet Death."

The grim humor possessed by Old Tom appeared on rare occasions. Once, I remember, the ladies of the staff, in a slack moment gathered together to discuss the intriguing question of diets. Ann West had recently embarked on the banana diet: four bananas for each meal, a glass of milk in between, and nothing else for 10 days. Verona Sanford had immense faith in the power of green vegetables, and so it went. Old Tom listened with grim attention and then, thumping the counter to add emphasis to his pronouncement, rasped out, "Wot I says is eat wot ya wants and when yer dead, yer dead!"

But somehow, why I do not know, it seemed that the most embarrassing situations and gaffes always occurred at the home of Mrs. Nesbitt at the extreme end of the South Run. Mrs. Nesbitt has vanished from the scene now but memories of her warm hospitality, her generosity, her kindliness, her humility, will remain with me for many years. "So let your Light shine before men" applies particularly to such as she. In the heat of summer, in the depth of winter, at midnight, at dawn, there was eternally a welcome and a haven for the sad, the hungry, and the weary beneath her roof. And why she should have been humiliated, embarrassed, persecuted (almost) by Old Tom can be regarded as one of those mysteries, those strange irregularities of our daily lives.

It must be mentioned here that the Nesbitts, while living in Toronto, had seen fit to adopt a boy and girl notwithstanding the fact that they had raised a fine family of their own. These two children, Doreen and Ronnie, were a perpetual reminder, a living proof, in fact of the ascendancy of heredity over environment. Both, as they grew older, seemed destined to hurtle down the Primrose Path with unprecedented speed. I remember them as eager, neatly dressed, attractive children, but only as children. As they developed, despite the sterling example of their foster-parents, they seemed to drift willingly, eagerly, into such sordid influences as the seamy side of village life could offer. Many tears and much heartbreak were suffered by Mr. and Mrs. Nesbitt in consequence and I fear that they reaped little reward from their altruism. But under all conditions, as I have suggested, it was never less than a pleasure to wheel the old Dodge along the Nesbitt driveway, fully aware of the kindly hospitality that awaited us.

On one such occasion on a blisteringly hot day in August, Old Tom and I laboured into the Nesbitt kitchen with the heavy load of groceries. Mrs. Nesbitt had been labouring outdoors in her garden. She, likewise, was hot, and the cooling drink she had prepared, together with cake and cookies, provided a welcome respite. As we sat at the kitchen table enjoying her bounty Mrs. Nesbitt remarked pleasantly, "Well, Mr. Marley, it's been so warm these last few days that I haven't been near the village, so you'll have to tell me all the news."

Tom straightened in his chair, glared at Mrs. Nesbitt, and answered grimly, "Don't you know there's a war on?" Mrs. Nesbitt, properly horrified (and thinking, perhaps, that the war was already on our frontier) said, "Oh Mr. Marley, surely not!" He replied, "Yes there is, there's a war on; planes flyin' over, droppin' bombs on them pore people, 'undreds of troops marchin' in."

Mrs. Nesbitt, suitably shocked, enquired. "Well, where is this war, Mr. Marley?"

There was a pause while Tom searched his memory but after a few grunts and swallows, he replied, "Where is it? Well, I'll tell ya, Mum. It's over in Urine, that's where it is, over in Urine. All them planes flyin' over, droppin' them bombs on them pore people. Oh, I tells ya, it's 'orrible."

Mrs. Nesbitt and I fought for composure and pondered as to which side was in the right, the American troops or the natives of Iran. I admit with some degree of shame that all other details of this particular skirmish in Iran have long been forgotten.

Another instance of Old Tom's skill with malapropisms is here related. Again at Mrs. Nesbitt's one dreary January afternoon we were offered the customary hospitality expressed in terms of tea and cake and a chance to rest for a few moments.

Again, Mrs. Nesbitt appealed to Tom for newsworthy items, and he replied bluntly, "Well, Mum, I've only 'eard one piece of news, and that ain't good. John's wife's dead!" Mrs. Nesbitt was swift with her concern. "Oh, Mr. Marley! Surely not! Poor Mrs. Carmichael! Why, I didn't even know she was ill. When did this happen?"

"Well, I don't know too much about it, mum, but I 'eard they took 'er into 'ospital three days ago, 'n then when I 'eard yesterday they was givin' 'er Hoxydol, I knowed there wasn't no 'ope!"

Though sobered by these grim tidings Mrs. Nesbitt and I exchanged glances, and immediately before my eyes there swam a vision of the aged and frail Mrs. Carmichael, supine within an oxygen tent, expiring beneath an enormous halo of detergent suds!

But perhaps the most excruciating impasses of all in relation to the Nesbitts transpired sometime later when the wayward Doreen, having dropped out of school, married a young lad in the Navy and produced, in short order, a strong and smiling child named Danny, returned, now and then, to stay for extended periods with her parents.

After one protracted stay of several months, it was rumored that the husband of Doreen had taken off for good, and apparently had departed for distant lands of the South Pacific to return no more.

This was not so surprising and was in fact the rule rather than the exception in such boy and girl alliances. But when, about a year afterwards, Doreen gave evidence of being plainly pregnant again, village tongues began to wag with a vengeance. Throughout the weeks that followed Doreen, now firmly established in her adopted-parents' home, maintained an admirable composure, seconded only by that of Mrs. Nesbitt. It remained, however, for Old Tom, with his direct, no-nonsense approach, to rush blindly in where more discreet angels feared to tread. Therefore, one sunny afternoon, urged by Mrs. Nesbitt to pause for a quick cup of tea, we had gathered around the hospitable table when Doreen, by now startlingly gravid, appeared briefly to announce that she was about to walk over to the village.

On several previous occasions, I had found Doreen's condition acutely embarrassing. At first, I had sought to avert my gaze; sometimes I had tried to pretend that she wasn't there, but as the weeks elapsed both attitudes became more infantile, since she was so definitely there; she loomed in the background, the foreground, and the middle distance like some monstrous pumpkin. No sooner had she departed from the house than Old Tom leaned forward with a conspiratorial air, and glared across the table at our hostess. I recognized the signs, but was not prepared for quite so blunt an attack. With the loud thump of clenched fist upon table, he asked, in three short words, the question that a score of housewives had longed but had not dared to ask. "WHERE'S 'ER 'USBAND?" Poor Mrs. Nesbitt, cowering in her chair, resembled a defenceless rabbit cornered by a ferret, but there was no escaping the scrutiny of the merciless eyes. She uttered a startled groan, contrived a few tears, (genuine, I am sure) and a handkerchief was produced and employed. At this point, I believe that Tom realized that perhaps he had gone too far. He made sympathetic noises and was about to speak, when Mrs. Nesbitt launched into a passionate and tearful defence of Doreen and as passionate a castigation of her son-in-law. ("He's no good, Mr. Marley, I tell you he's no good, leaving that poor girl all alone, and…")

In the end, peace of a sort was restored, and Old Tom sought to offer comforting words and sustaining phrases, such as "Well, that's 'ow it goes, Mum, and y'gotta take the rough with the smooth is what I says," but the heart knows its own grief, and I fear his homilies went unheeded. When we were safely on our way once more, with much food for thought, Tom delivered himself of the following terse pronouncement. "Mrs. Nesbitt says as 'ow 'e's no good; it's the girl's the one as is no good, not 'im. Seemed like a decent enough guy to me. Well, that's 'ow she goes."

Later, of course, Doreen went away while the Nesbitt parents bravely carried on and perhaps a month passed before we were privileged to enter upon a nativity scene of sorts. Doreen, in no way embarrassed by the recent blessed event, urged us to view the new arrival; Mrs. Nesbitt, too, seemed to sustain the role of proud grandmother to perfection. And Old Tom, glaring down with fierce disapproval at the slumbering infant, delivered himself of yet another faux pas. "Does the gov'mint pay ya five dollars a month for this one, same as for 'im?" he demanded, pointing to young Danny, (as if the baby had three heads and thus was beyond the pale). To Doreen's affirmative, he said sagely, "Well, that's right, mum, so they oughter; you take it, mum, always take all ya kin git off the gov'mint, 'cause they'll take it offa you every time they kin."

As the months progressed, somehow, the Nesbitt family adjusted to the stresses and strains of life, but Old Tom became gradually more silent and morose. His movements became slower, his gait more laboured. I would notice him brooding in odd corners sometimes mumbling to himself. Once he confided in me, "The boss is 'intin' that me time's about up, I kin expec' me walking papers any day. Well, Trivver, I tells 'im, 'That's all right with me, Ken,' I says, 'Any time you wants me to move on, I'm ready.' I never was be'olden to nobody, but I tells ya straight, Trivver, 'e'll regret it; 'e'll regret it. There ain't many men my age kin do 'alf of what I does. But that suits me fine; when 'e says the word, I'll move on!"

And so, at last, word was passed about one morning that this was to be Old Tom's last day. I think he would have welcomed some form of recognition on the part of the staff, some small tribute for what he believed was years of faithful service, of work well and truly done. But none was forthcoming because for most of us his departure was hailed with relief. To me, he mumbled something like, "Well, Trivver, guess you won't be seein' me around 'ere no more. But I got no regrets, I'm willin' to go. And I got plenty to do in me garden, all them blackberry vines to cut out, 'n Mrs. Gordon's arter me to mow 'er lawn, 'n doctor wants me to cut 'is 'edge. Oh, I got lots ter keep me busy, I tells ya. 'N' if ya needs 'elp any time, y'only got ter say so."

Thus Old Tom passed from the daily scene and I saw him seldom thereafter. Occasionally, as I passed by in the Dodge, going South, or going North, I might see his resolute form, plodding along the sidewalk looking neither to right nor left gazing at the ground ahead, but there was seldom an opportunity for me to stop and chat. When he had been gone for some weeks a remorse of sorts, or a sense of guilt developed among us. We began to wish that we had, after all, done something nice for Old Tom or made him a presentation and vague plans were laid in that direction.

Some time and thought was spent in deciding what he might like, or what might be suitable, but inspiration seemed notably lacking. After all, there was little that Tom didn't already have; television, radio, a well-stocked wardrobe: he had them all; he didn't read, he no longer smoked; a bottle of some alcoholic beverage somehow didn't seem enough, (and besides this would have incurred the violent opposition of Mrs. Marley.) Also, there existed the delicate situation of the nature of the gift; it must be personal, it could not be something whereby his wife might benefit.

And so the weeks dragged by until someone would remember "We've got to do something about Tom's present," and then recriminations and indecisions would arise again. Finally, it was decided that a floor lamp would be suitable, a tasteful but modest floor lamp, beside which Tom could sit of an evening to watch television or to leaf through the newspaper. By this time, though, there was little joy in the act of giving, I fear, and it was with some difficulty that a collection was made for there was indecision over the amount that each staff member should contribute. Some doubted if Tom were really worth what others were ready and willing to give.

In the end, however, differences were resolved, and the floor lamp, burnished and splendid, arrived. Tom was summoned late one afternoon to the Emporium, on some vague pretext, but the ceremony, if such it might be termed, was not convincing. There was no Master of Ceremonies to render a befitting speech for too many months had elapsed since Tom's departure and he, I am sure, was well aware of this. He accepted our belated tribute with gruff gratitude but without spontaneity. He had, I know, expected "something better", and he could not have been impressed, nor pleased, by the unpardonable delay. And thereafter we saw little of him, in or around the Emporium.

Then perhaps a year later, while Mrs. Marley was making an extended visit to Vancouver, Old Tom was snatched away. To meet his Maker? To the Elysian Fields? Who can truly say? But the end was sudden and swift, and I am sure, as he would have wished it to be. ("When me time's up, Trivver, I wants it to be quick-like; no layin' around in the 'ospital sufferin' fer me; git it over with quick, I says!") And thus it was. I do not remember if the staff sent a deputy to attend the funeral services at Duncan. A wreath of roses, yes; but that I think was all. (I remembered having heard Tom say, more than once, "Did y'ave a good time at the funeral, Trivver? Was there a good crowd? Oh, ya didn't go arter all?" and then, with reproach, "I would 'a went me-self, but I 'ad work to do at 'ome, but I thought *you* would 'a went!") And I remember one of our staff remarking, "Oh, poor Old Tom! I hear he's going to be cremated, with all that lovely white hair, what a shame!"

And so it is; or *"C'est la vie"*. If there is a moral to be read into the Life of Old Tom, it escapes me. But there is ample room for conjecture, to wonder what lay behind the impenetrable mask. He was kindly and generous upon occasion while other times he was blunt, sometimes even uncouth and irascible, and certainly infuriating. But was not this simply a mask to conceal his self-doubt, indecision, and insecurity that surely lay beneath? He was critical but he could be fiercely loyal.

And who is to say what he might or might not have been if he had not been a victim of World War One, if he had married another, if he had attained the advantages of an education, if perhaps he had not been drawn into the melting-pot of the Emporium?

The prefix that might be attached to a summary of any life: IF?

The Woman who Became a Bird

*W*ho is there, among our generation, to whom the magical name of Yma Sumac is utterly without meaning? Surely there are those who remember as if it were yesterday that far-off night when her voice was first heard through the medium of radio and history was made? But listen now to what the world has to say concerning this amazing woman.

"There is no voice like it in the world of music today," says Glenn Dillard Gunn of the *Washington Times-Herald*. "It has a greater range than any female voice of concert or opera. It soars into the acoustic stratosphere or it plumbs sub-contralto depths of pitch with equal ease. Such voices happen only once in a generation." In Buenos Aires, *La Prensa* said, "The greatest musical revelation of our times." In Rio de Janeiro, *O Globo* commented, "Sumac dominates the artistic sensibilities of all Brazil with her magic and divine voice. The problems of our modern world are forgotten through the magnetism of this fabulous gift, which comes to us, directly descended from Atahualpa, last of the Inca kings." And in Los Angeles, Albert Goldberg of the *Times* said, "to hear her weave that fantastic counterpoint over the complex rhythms of her accompaniment is at last to experience something new in music."

Small wonder then that in the mysterious land of the Incas, Yma Sumac assumed an almost deified position as "The Bird Who Became a Woman", and "The Voice of the Earthquake".

No one in her native village of Ichochan, 16,000 feet high in the Andes of Peru had ever heard such a voice in human form when this "chosen maiden" sang at their annual festivals to the sun.

No one in the big cities below had heard such a voice, either. So when exciting rumours of her rare talent and beauty reached officials of the Peruvian government, they arranged to bring Yma Sumac down to the coastlands, a decision that almost caused an uprising among some 30,000 upland Peruvians over the loss of their revered ritual singer.

In the first public concert held, I believe, in New York, Yma Sumac specialized in the interpretation of a series of ancient Inca themes gleaned from a tribal legend known as "the Xtabay".

But in all this burnished facade stray cracks appeared. A friend of mine, ever vigilant, had it upon the highest authority that the fabulous singer came, not from the high Andes, but from the purlieus of The Bronx where she was known by the innocuous name of Amy Camus and where she sang originally in a humble church choir.

And years later, as her meteoric career began to falter, unsavory gossip trickled into the Los Angeles *Times*, covering an unseemly public brawl in the streets where one Moises Vivanco, her husband, and a jealous lover engaged in battle while Yma Sumac cowered behind the trunk of a palm tree.

And still later, when this adverse publicity had been forgotten, a brave attempt at a comeback was noted. What came next, so far as I know is silence but yet to many the name, and the memory of the amazing voice still spells enchantment.

And what has all this to do with us? We, natives of the Cowichan Valley have our legends, too, and we guard them closely. To us, another name, less fanciful perhaps, conjures up many memories. This is the name of Elsie Kirby, which is well known among us. For Elsie, like Yma Sumac, possessed a voice which was heard throughout the land and which derived a fair measure of merit for its owner.

For the uninformed, it must be known that Elsie and her schoolteacher husband, Girard (hereinafter referred to as Gird) arrived in our valley a number of years ago, and before long she had embarked on the first stages of a career, that, in a relative way, paralleled that of Miss Sumac.

She sang to begin with in a church choir and at times offered her services as soloist. She sang at weddings: such durable items as "O Promise Me", "The Wedding Prayer", and "I Love You Truly". She won praise and acclaim at village concerts and amateur nights and she joined the Lake Cowichan Music Club, which to some degree furthered her cause. In later years, she formed and conducted a group known as the Lake Cowichan Chorale. She was her own press agent and with the confidence and exuberance of youth, considerable drive, and ambition, she accomplished minor miracles.

The measure of her success might be judged by the observant from the hue of her hair, which, in its original state, was a simple brown. As the years passed, adding triumph upon triumph, a golden glint appeared, spread, blazed into a yellow brilliance, faded to paler hues, then paler yet, until in the final stages, an impressive aureole of silver remained. The calibre of her songs, too, suffered change. Schmaltzy ballads and ornithological lyrics were discarded in favour of art songs, of arias from Mozart, from "The Messiah", and from the vast storehouse of Bach and Schubert. But despite her success Elsie maintained a becoming modesty before her wide circle.

To an erudite musician-friend of mine, she once made this alarming statement: "I can't read a note of music, but I have perfect pitch," leaving my friend with much food for thought.

Naturally, perhaps, though regrettably, as Elsie Kirby's career progressed to more exalted realms a faint condescension became evident, a tendency at times to "blame with faint praise."

"Oh, Yma Sumac," (she might say), "Oh yes, it's an amazing voice. But she's using an echo chamber, of course. I could tell that right away." Or: "Oh yes, I heard her last night in *Lucia di Lammermoor*. Poor Lily Pons. I really felt sorry for her when she cracked on that high E flat." Or: "I bought this recording of Maria Callas singing *Rigoletto* the other day and I thought she did it really well in spots if you *like* a coloratura voice. I can't say I care for them myself." And: "I'm really making progress with the professor now. Of course between you and me, he's no musician, but he really does try."

My associations with Elsie, through the auspices of our local music club, were not unpleasant. Her confidence in herself could not fail to rub off a little upon her accompanist of the moment, and her cheery, "Well, don't worry. I know we'll get through it somehow" was to some degree comforting. Like Yma Sumac, she, too, had a few detractors in her audience: those who smiled knowingly when they believed her to be singing a shade off key, those who tittered audibly at a music club meeting when she announced as one of her numbers, the haunting, nostalgic Rachmaninoff "O Cease Thy Singing, Maiden Fair, Those Songs of Georgian Land".

Apart from the exalted world of music, other contact with Elsie was established in the mundane world of Gordon Stores where for years I had from time to time attended to her wants and had answered the telephone a score of times to hear her memorable voice announce:

"Elsie Kirby speaking. Is that you, Trevor? I have a little order here that I'd like delivered today, please. I'll just read it through. Let's see, two loaves of bread, no, make it three, a pound of Nabob coffee, two pounds of Mom's margarine, and a box of soda crackers, the salted ones, not the plain, and a lettuce, and a medium-size cabbage. Now about meat. How about a pot roast, about five pounds (Gird always likes that) and a pound of bacon. Oh yes, and could you cut off *all* the rind and slice it really thin? I know it's putting you to a lot of extra work, but...oh yes, and oranges, a dozen oranges, and I don't like to complain but last time there were three bad ones. Perhaps you could do something about that. Did I say eggs? Well, two dozen eggs and now I think, I *think* that's everything. Just send it over this afternoon and thanks a lot."

It should be noted, perhaps, that Elsie's husband, Gird, did not share his wife's musical talents. He frankly confessed he didn't like her type of music or her way of singing and always managed to absent himself from Elsie's musical soirées. He was a huge man, with the shoulders of a wrestler.

As the years drifted past, Elsie's choir gained in stature and in reputation and in later years she allied her talents to those of the Duncan Operatic Society securing coveted roles as a statuesque Merry Widow and a bouncy Countess Maritza.

But before this stage in her career had been reached, there occurred an incident, an episode that has given me much pause for contemplation. It began innocuously enough with a telephone call to the House of Gordon, the content of which was approximately as follows:

"Gordon Stores? Elsie Kirby speaking. Is that you, Trevor? I have a few things here I'd like you to send over just a little order, ready? Three loaves of bread, one brown, a medium cabbage, and a jar of sweet pickles, the 16-ounce size, I think, and lemons, a half a dozen, I think, and potatoes, the new ones, not the old, yes, a five pound bag will be fine. And prunes, yes, a two pound bag. Now I think that's everything. And, oh yes, Trevor, when you come to the house, just call in, because I'd like to go over the Rachmaninoff accompaniment with you. Yes, the song Wylie wants us to do, "In the Silence of the Night". I'd like to go over the phrasing with you and perhaps we should work out some tempo changes. I'll be in all afternoon anyway because I'm resting my voice for tomorrow night. See you later then, goodbye."

Some two hours later, perhaps, I halted before the Kirby residence on Larch Street in the exclusive residential area of Parkstone [the official name of the Hundred Houses]. This abode had in its original form been indistinguishable from a dozen similar homes but like its chatelaine, over the years, it, too, had gained in prestige. A picture-window had been added to its facade, as well as a veneer of pink stucco, and a carport in the rear sheltered Gird's yellow Oldsmobile, plus a welter of fishing equipment and children's toys.

Over the long years of servitude at Gordon's Emporium, I have learned that much can be discovered of human nature from the condition of the back porch of the housewife. Not the front porch, which is invariably swept and garnished, and tidied, to present a convincing show to the passing world.

But in the confines of the sheltered back porch are revealed the inner conflicts of the inmates. The slings and arrows of outrageous fortune come to rest there and many are the battles lost and won over the establishment of law and order.

Such were my thoughts as I toiled up the steep and littered stairs that led to the Kirby back porch, where a hodgepodge of shoes and gumboots, old brooms and mops were intermingled with a cardboard carton half filled with empty tins and a part sack of rotting potatoes. But this is unfair and unkind. What do I know of the back porches of the Yma Sumacs, the Maria Callases, the Kirsten Flagstads of this world? And after all, does it matter in the final analysis? Surely it does not.

To my polite but firm knock on the back door there was no response nor was there to my second attempt. Elsie had *said* she would be at home all afternoon "resting her voice" so, emboldened, I opened the door and called out in hearty tones, "Hi there. Anyone at home?"

Still no response. Of course, Elsie could be asleep, or she might be conceivably in the bathroom, and anyhow, I couldn't continue to stand on the threshold, bawling out, "Anyone home?" In the kitchen there prevailed a sort of controlled confusion: a mound of unwashed dishes had overflowed from the kitchen sink onto the table near the window, but a small space remained free, and there lay the copy of the Rachmaninoff art song, "In the Silence of the Night", with the name Wylie S. Grant written across the title page. Near at hand was a small writing pad and a ballpoint pen. Had Elsie left a written message explaining her absence? Well, there was a message of sorts but only notes concerning the song: "See phrasing of bars 17 to 24; build up tempo to climax on page 3, bars 42 to 49", "Discuss the inner meaning of the introduction". No, there was no clue there.

Next, I experimented with my brother's solution in such perplexed moments: the discreet but emphatic cough, but this brought no result, nor did another appeal, "Hi there, Elsie. Anyone at home?" This left no alternative but to unpack the bag of groceries and make my departure.

But as I began to unload the carton and enlarge the free area on the table to receive the groceries my attention was caught by a vague rustling from some obscure source near the floor. I could not recall a cat or puppy at any time in the Kirby ménage, and the idea of a mouse or rat was unthinkable. The rustle increased, and next I heard a low note, a croak or a faint squawk. What could this mean? Forgetting the groceries, I peered beneath the table and there beheld, to my mounting consternation, a small and scraggly and tousled chicken, that is to say it resembled a chicken more than any other fowl, the sort of chicken that one might see feebly scratching for insects in a dusty knoll in the uncivilized areas of darkest Africa. I gazed down at the shabby bird, which slowly shuffled out from the shadows uttering now and then a mournful, questioning note.

Desperately I tried to resolve the situation. What was I to do? Elsie must have gone out. Somehow the wretched bird had sneaked in but surely it could not be left at liberty in the kitchen. Well I remembered the irate tones of a Mrs. Alexander, who years before, had berated me over the telephone at Gordon's: "Say, what's the idea? Your delivery man left the door open and a bloody big dog got in the house and cleaned up half the roast and knocked the eggs and milk on the floor. You'd better make it good and bring another roast over right away quick before Sam gets in to supper or I'll quit and start dealing at Scholey's and I mean it!"

Surely then, the way lay clear before me. The offending bird must be thrown out. I could not allow such a situation to arise wherein Elsie, telephoning the store, would with reason complain of the ineptness of the grocery man in allowing a hen to get into her kitchen and peck away at the bread and potatoes and despoil Cousin Wylie's Rachmaninoff.

But as I stooped down beneath the table to lure the bird to come forward, again it uttered a mournful, questioning note and shook its draggled plumage.

And on this instant, in the words of the poet: "Sudden a Thought Came Like a Full Blown Rose". Was it? Could it be?

Again the plaintive questioning tone from beneath the table. And now there could be no doubt. I was convinced. Elsie then had eclipsed, had even transcended, the immortal Yma Sumac legend. She had deified herself as "the woman who became a bird". How could there be room for doubt?

And I, a humble store clerk, had witnessed or almost witnessed the miracle. With wakening interest and amazement I regarded the bird which slowly came forward into the light. Yes, surely yes and yet?

Perhaps the transfiguration had come upon Elsie before she had been able to change from her workaday attire. This would explain the general untidiness, the air of neglect that surrounded her glorification. The top of the head? Well, it *was* whitish, silvery, perhaps. The profile? I remembered that certain of her scathing sisterhood had described Elsie's profile as birdlike, her nose as that of a hawk, an unfair criticism of course. The legs, the feet? When had I last scrutinized Elsie's legs? Those of the bird were scaly and yellow, the feet and claws none too clean, but the trusting advance, the mournful confiding note: no, one could no longer doubt.

But still, in her new form, Elsie could create untold havoc. Unquestionably the bird was hungry. If left unguarded in the kitchen, the bread, the potatoes, the cabbage even would not long remain undamaged and I would be blamed. No, the bird (Elsie) must be caught and hustled outside forthwith.

However, as I reached forward with outstretched hands fresh doubts assailed me. If, as the result of an incredible miracle, this bedraggled bird *were* really Elsie, had I after all the legal right to oust her from her home? Supposing, in the wilderness of the back yard, a cat espied her or what if a neighbour dog "got" her? Mine would be the guilt as surely as if it had been my hand that struck her down. As if aware of my thoughts, Elsie (the bird) retreated beneath the kitchen stove, still rustling her (its) soiled plumage. And again I was pursued by doubts. If Elsie had been chosen to attain this miracle, this transmigration, surely she would have revealed herself as, well, a bird of paradise, a nightingale, a mockingbird, anything rather than this untidy bundle of feathers. But then this may have been the "first time". Perhaps, as in a form of evolution, further experiment would produce more exalted results. Perhaps, next time. The movement of a dirty yellowish foot from beneath the stove brought me back to earth and to the knowledge that action must come quickly.

Supposing I grabbed the bird with both hands and threw it out of the door. Need anyone be the wiser? What if, however, Elsie were suddenly to return to human form? How would I feel, what could I say, if she returned to the flesh as I dragged her out from beneath the open oven door? Suppose at that precise moment her children were to return from school as well they might? Supposing, even worse, if Gird and his gargantuan frame were to lumber over the threshold as I groveled with Elsie on the floor? No, it was not to be thought of; my way lay clear once more, for only escape was possible. Firmly I placed the bag of potatoes, the lemons, and the sweet pickles on the table, picked up the carton, cast one glance at the drooping head and yellow legs beneath the stove and closed the door hearing as I did again the low reproachful note. With a mind too full for thought, with a brain too bewildered to reason, I resumed my seat in the old grey Dodge truck and continued on my way.

Some weeks later, at a soirée presented by the Music Club, I related the foregoing account with perhaps a few minor embellishments. It produced the anticipated mirth but as the laughter mounted, I began to feel a burning sense of guilt. As I had built to a climax I glanced across at Elsie resplendent in her party finery, a low-cut ice-blue gown, her burnished hair agleam with jewels, did I detect a pleading look, an involuntary movement of her scarlet lips as if to say: "No, no, not here. Don't betray my secret, not here." But this may well be imagination. Or was there tension and dissembling in her attitude as she explained, "Oh, that damned old chicken. It was given to Ritchie by one of his school chums and Gird's going to wring its neck one of these days."

But to few of us, in a long lifetime, is given the rare privilege of witnessing such miracles. For those who have, again the words of the poet are relevant: "Close your eyes in holy dread, and weave a circle round him thrice, for he on honey dew has fed, and drunk the milk of paradise."

The Fire at the High School: January 1964

*I*n addition to his stories, Trevor Green also maintained extensive journals throughout his life. These handwritten treasure troves contain many details that will interest the reader of today, and none more, surely, than his notes about the terrible fire of Jan. 21, 1964, that many Lake Cowichan residents still living in the area will well remember. Here is an excerpt from his journal of that month.

Jan. 21: *Quel jour, mais quel jour!* What an understatement!! The morning passed in tranquil fashion: tidying up the woodshed; in the afternoon, I was adjusting the leaking tap in the bathroom when Yvonne [who had been doing some substitute teaching that day] drove in, honking furiously and yelling, "The high school's on fire!!"

Tony was home that day and the two of us raced for the car; at the railway track [at the west end of Greendale Road], we saw a huge billow of black smoke like an atomic explosion cloud.

On reaching the hill above the elementary school we saw the roof of the auditorium and home ec room dissolve in flames. What a spectacle! Children's parents, and fire department personnel were rushing hither and yon. Rain and snow were alternately descending [and added to the confusion of] cars, hoses, pandemonium, and rumours of all sorts. I helped remove furniture from the Saywells' abode.

Yvonne returned with Kathy and hot tea and cookies.

The gym, auditorium, and home ec room were by now a welter of flame with the roof blazing and smoke pouring forth. Fire trucks from Duncan, Honeymoon Bay, Youbou, and Mesachie Lake were all doing noble work.

I stayed till 5:30 p.m. The east wing by now was safe but for water damage. I returned at 7 p.m. with the children to collect Kathy's books and coat, etc. but was not allowed in and so quitted the building.

The west front was still ablaze despite seven or eight hoses. A veritable creek was flowing down to South Shore Road. People, cars, children, and dogs were there en masse. Rumours of every sort were flying about. I got home again about 9 p.m. and had one closing thought: "Man the inventive is no match for nature the mighty."

Jan. 22: We visited the painful scene of the ruin at 9 a.m. Mr. Clode was really kind and took Kathy to the classroom and locker room to recover her possessions. Her coat and shoes reeked of smoke, her books were undamaged, but her zipper case was the worse for wear and water. We returned to find Mr. Hobson had kindly engaged my services as night watchman to start at 8 p.m. Consequently I napped after lunch to equalize night and day, which I now consider fruitless. I met Earl La Forge at the maintenance shop and was briefed as to my duties by William Budd. The duties are not onerous: to consist of patrolling the ruins at intervals till dawn, employing hoses as deemed necessary. And to refill the kerosene blower underground where transformers are located. Encountered L. Plater, E. Towle, Wadsworth Electric personnel (of Duncan), and J. F. T. Saywell, the latter in a pathetic state of near somnambulism.

The Wadsworth Electric spokesman was convinced that the cause stemmed from other than electrical frailties. So be it. But results all the same.

What of the night? It was far shorter than I had dared to anticipate. It was pleasantly warm in the maintenance shop with chocolate bars for the asking, day-old sandwiches, and aged fruitcake ditto. Earl La Forge was a very affable co-watchman. We filled the blower with kerosene several times and patrolled the premises frequently.

Frost started at midnight. It was shades of Cowper: "The frost performs its silent ministry, unhelped by any wind."

We quenched stubborn flame in pit of the ruins with fire hoses and locked the outer doors of Stanley Gordon School, which had been overlooked. We also brewed instant tea on a hotplate. It was very bad tea. I cannot recommend same. I was relieved at 7:30 a.m. by William Budd and was able to enjoy a glorious dawn sky, with sun on the snow-covered hills. Too, too lovely. And so home.

Jan. 23: I napped fitfully until noon; Yvonne was teaching at Paldi. Nice day with almost a trace of sun. I conserved my energies for night duty at the school with gentle labours at woodboxes, and splitting kindling. Today was also my first immersion in the river of the season: frigid but with an immense sense of well-being as a result. [Editor's note: Trevor Green loved these refreshing dips in the Cowichan River at all seasons.] Off to school at 8 p.m. This time it was an endless night despite tea, coke, potato chips, and a midnight snack. Rain and wet snow were still descending. The ruins of the school were very eerie. Earl La Forge and I dozed fitfully between our duties. Conversation flagged but a bond of friendship well established, one trusts. I was relieved at dawn by Garry Anderson, later by Gordon Erickson. Home before 8 a.m.

Jan 24: Rain and wet snow. Arrived at school at 8 p.m. Soon visited by Garry Anderson who conducted me on a grand tour of the premises. There are now four heaters to fill. Later I was visited by William Budd, who divulged "The Story of My Life" until 12:30 a.m. With reservations, that was very interesting. I had access to a piano, which was certainly a diversion, and there were also facilities to heat soup in that classroom. Dozed fitfully on the classroom floor; the roar of a space heater is not conducive to slumber. I was greeted at 8 a.m. by Anderson. It was a glorious morning.

Jan 26: I dozed in bed till 10:30 a.m. but could not sleep thereafter for the sun was too alluring. I left for the school at 4:30 p.m. where I was briefed by Budd. I mopped up the floor of the sewing room where the ceiling tile was falling down, also Room 7, I think. Then I returned to H.Q. in Room 1. I had a visit from Erickson as well as Hunter Construction. The piano was a tremendous boon. Yvonne, Kathy, and Tony arrived with supper at 7 p.m. Tony stayed till 9. I read, and played piano till midnight. However, the night's relief did not arrive. I phoned: no dice and so was confronted by an eight hour vigil. I stoked the heaters and dozed on the floor from 2 a.m. until 4:30. I resolved then and there that night watchmen must be a breed apart and the least of them worthy of their hire. Alan McBride appeared at 8 a.m. to take over. Home, breakfast and so to bed.

Jan. 27: Wet and dreary again. Up betimes (6 a.m.) to be at school at 8 a.m. and found indescribable confusion but beneath all this perhaps a sort of order. In company with Reid Harvey and Garry Anderson, I drove the Gordon Stores truck to Youbou for desks. Took some desks to the IWA Hall (being converted into three classrooms), some to the Anglican Church (three classrooms) and some to the United Church (four classrooms).

Carpenters, electricians, and plumbers were swarming all over the ruins, a cleaning squad was indoors. I also went to Hillcrest [Lumber at Mesachie Lake] for a load of 8x8 timbers (specially cut) on which to rest three mobile classrooms brought expressly from Vancouver.

It's quite wonderful, really, how organizations have banded together to help an appalling situation.

William Budd also informed me that I can look forward to a year of steady work with the school board, which is very encouraging news.

The Trial

*F*rom the vantage point of my desk on the mezzanine of Gordon's Emporium, I saw, with some misgiving, Constable Bardswell approach with measured tread, followed at a respectful distance by Henry J. Greer, game warden. Their presence reminded me, all too painfully, of the occasion when Bardswell had found it necessary to produce a cheque of mine returned from the bank at Duncan with sinister letters N.S.F. written thereon. The police officer had been very nice about it, but still the embarrassment remained for a long time to come.

But I need not have worried, for "Pokey" Bardswell merely required my help in identifying a number of household objects which had been discovered in the hideaway of one Fredric B., and which were believed to have been lifted from the abode of my late Aunt Doll. Therefore, when a brief leave of absence had been granted me, I went out into the bright March sunshine, escorted to the police car by the two gendarmes. As we drove out of town toward the swampy area where B. dwelt, Cst. Bardswell related how several of the summer cottages down river had been ransacked and rifles, fishing rods, and other valuable articles had been stolen. In due course, his suspicions had been confirmed, and these items, including Aunt Doll's effects, had reappeared in the hovel. The miscreant, it seemed, was a furtive, shifty-eyed creature, variously employed in sawmills and logging camps.

I had seen him about the village driving an Overland 4 of indeterminate vintage, but beyond a vague impression of pale thin cheeks, a scratchy moustache and restless darting eyes, nothing else had registered.

Bardswell parked his car by the roadside and the three of us crossed over to the edge of the swamp, which so effectively screened the humble abode from the gaze of the intruder. The morning sun was fast melting the thin skim of ice which coated the mud, but the spring rains had raised the level of the swamp, so that Fred's roof, like an abandoned beaver house, poked out above the welter of scrub willow and hardback perhaps one hundred yards from where we stood.

But the law is seldom lacking in resource. From a nearby pile of discarded bridge planking the worthy constable dragged several long boards to the water's edge. By throwing two of these in advance and walking out upon them, then dragging two more from behind and repeating the operation, we edged our way across the swamp while water and mud oozed about our shoes. Upon reaching the rickety shack, Bardswell pulled aside a few boards which served in lieu of a door and we squeezed our way within.

The litter and confusion that met our eyes was indescribable. Mounds of crumpled newspapers, stacks of mildewed magazines, heaps of rusted tin cans, bottles of every size and condition, bundles of wood, scraps of bark, torn and trampled paper cartons, these were but a few recognizable items in the great private collection of Fredric B. By pulling aside a few battered wall boards, Cst. Bardswell unearthed a rifle, several sections of fishing-rod, and some of Aunt Doll's possessions: an old camera, nutcrackers, an ashtray, and a few bits of Devon pottery that I recognized at once.

We surveyed this conglomeration with the respect it merited and pondered over the unknown and hidden forces that dominate the lives of men. What impulses had transformed B.? What were the childhood influences that now compelled him in maturity to become a scavenger who crept furtively at night to the garbage pails, the trash piles, the empty homes of his kind? Heredity or environment, which was responsible? These, and other questions were discussed while the gendarmes smoked, and I admired the wasteland of mud, water, March wind, and sunshine as seen from holes in the shattered boards which served for windows in Fredric's morning-room.

With mingled feelings we picked our way back across the lurching muddy planks, which fell with a loud smack into the water as the constable bravely hurled them in advance. Upon having returned to the store, Greer informed me that I would be notified well in advance of the date of the trial and that my aid in securing the services of a certain Mrs. Henshawe (Aunt Doll's sister) as a material witness would be greatly valued. Thus I returned to my desk with its litter of sales-tickets and ledgers with much food for thought.

That night I conversed by telephone with Mrs. Henshawe (Aunt Mabel). She might best be described as a pseudo-genteel demi-mondaine, who was part owner of a somewhat down-at-heel private hotel in a quiet and respectable section of Victoria.

Her husband had long been dead, her son had left for life in the Royal Canadian Navy, her arthritis was acute, her dentures were ill-fitting, her voice a rasping croak. Yet these defects aside, her life was not, in a way, without its compensations. Through the montage of the years she had dabbled with photography, oil-painting, Christian Science, lesser known cults, and the pursuit of Inner Cosmic Energy. Bridge, novels, and occasional dances or movies were her recreation; the hotel and its successful administration were her business. Her smile, a rather painful exposure of overlarge chalk-white teeth, and her laugh, a husky cackling, testified to her ready sense of humor. Her response to my proposition was favorable. She would be able and ready to appear at the trial whenever required, and would be delighted to revisit her rural haunts again after a long absence.

The next day, Cst. Bardswell told me that the trial was slated for the following Thursday afternoon. He murmured that Mrs. Henshawe might expect a government refund to cover travelling expenses. I was granted two hours reprieve from work for the appointed day so that I might personally chauffeur Aunt Mabel from the station in Duncan.

The day of the trial dawned clear and sunny. The March wind rustled the dried maple leaves along the roadside and swayed the silver-grey alder branches as I set out for Duncan. I looked closely along the moist ditches for the first dandelion and saw one, blazing like a newly-minted coin.

Aunt Mabel descended rheumatically from the train and hobbled across the platform to meet me. Her smile, a white gash between her thin, rouged cheeks was radiant. She was eager to appear at the trial, she croaked, and explained that she had borrowed her sister-in-law's black sealskin cloak for the occasion. This ancient garment hung from her shoulders in folds, and drooped about her bony legs. True to her family, all of whom were afflicted with a defective sense of color, she had pinned to the coat an enormous Woolworth American Beauty rose of velour. This, with her late sister's pearl earrings, completed the sum of accessories for the well-dressed witness.

On the way home Aunt Mabel's croaking voice prattled gaily. She hadn't heard from her son for several months, convoys on the Atlantic were daily being blown sky high, Paris would surely fall, her arthritis was progressively worse, but her wheezing laugh and wintry smile proved that life still had its humorous side. At lunch with my parents she chatted of old days, old friends, and the last days of Aunt Doll. At two o'clock we drove off in state to the trial.

We parked opposite the combined courthouse-and-jail, which was housed in a modest brown-painted building, barely larger than the smallest hen house. Aunt Mabel and I, unused to courthouse procedure, sat in the car, uncertain as to the next move. We were not sure whether we should enter the courthouse or wait until we were summoned. Beside the door, several cars were parked.

Some time had passed, the door opened and Cst. Bardswell, immaculate in his best uniform beckoned us in with an expansive gesture. Aunt Mabel shook out the folds of her sealskin cloak, adjusted her rose, and together we walked across to the courthouse. Upon entering, we looked about apprehensively for seating space. Directly in front of us sat Col. A.J. Dawson, magistrate, a small, thin, wiry man with a red face and blue eyes, looking not unlike a hungry and infuriated monkey. Behind him stood, in official pose, constables Greer and Bardswell. Beyond them a door led into the jail where presumably the prisoner languished. To the right of the entrance, partly concealed behind the half-open door, sat the court stenographer, Mrs. Greer, attired in a modest dark costume, her sober, earnest face and gold-rimmed glasses partially hidden beneath her wide-brimmed hat. Her small desk held a bottle of ink, a calendar, and her notebook. Below a little window stood a narrow bench. Aunt Mabel permitted herself to be guided thence and settled back drawing the folds of sealskin regally about her. I squeezed myself into the space beside her. In truth, it could now be said the court was full.

At this point I noticed a tall, well-dressed man, not wholly unknown to me, who had been concealed behind the now closed door. He was I knew not one of the villagers but of the rarer breed of summer visitors who owned lake and river property, and was present undoubtedly to recover his rods and fishing gear, which Fredric B. had added to his spoils. (For the present purpose he shall be called Mr. Dennison). He now leaned against the wall, looking aloof and bored, but anxious, none the less, for justice.

Col. Dawson now cleared his throat with a harsh rasp. "Call in the prisoner," he barked. Mrs. Greer's pencil scratched across her pad. Cst. Bardswell disappeared into the jail, and returned ten seconds later with Fredric B., who, like some rodent dragged from its burrow, blinked and twitched in the glare of public gaze. In the guise of prisoner or otherwise, he could in no way be termed picturesque.

He was neither tall nor short, fat nor lean, clad in shabby work clothes, unshaven, hair unkempt, shifty of eye, odorous of person; I felt convinced that his cause would evoke no sympathy from the assembled court. Led forth by Cst. Bardswell, he took his stand perhaps three feet from where I crouched on my bench.

There followed an interchange of question and reply between Col. Dawson and Mr. Dennison, who identified beyond all possible doubt as his two rifles and one fishing rod, also one gaudy calendar decorated with a portrait of an unclad lady desperately contriving to conceal her state of nature with a skipping rope. When this was displayed before our gaze Mr. Dennison appeared embarrassed and uncomfortable, while Aunt Mabel laughed harshly. "Silence in the Court," yelled the Colonel. This established, Mr. Dennison agreed to collect his belongings the next day and departed with evident relief.

Col. Dawson next probed the courtroom with fierce eyes. "Call Mrs. Henshawe," he barked at Cst. Bardswell, who turned to Aunt Mabel, not 10 feet distant, and requested that she rise. For a moment she was, as has been said of others, the cynosure of all eyes, those of the prisoner included. Col. Dawson cleared his throat again and rubbed his bony hands together. "Mrs. Henshawe," he said, "you have been called into court today to aid us in identifying certain articles believed to have been stolen from the home of your late sister. Do you hereby promise to tell the truth, the whole truth, and nothing but the truth, so help you God?" With this he pushed a tattered bible across to her. Aunt Mabel kissed it with obvious distaste and croaked out an affirmative, whereupon the Colonel turned to Cst. Greer. "Bring in Exhibit One," he ordered.

Cst. Greer retired into the jail and returned momently with a battered teapot that brought to my mind an intimate childhood picture of Aunt Doll's warm cosy kitchen. It was held for all to see. "What is this object, Mrs. Henshawe?" demanded the magistrate. Aunt Mabel narrowed her gaze, and peered attentively at Exhibit One. "That," she croaked, savoring her words, "is my sister's teapot." The Colonel appeared to feel some doubt. "Are you certain?" he asked. "Yes," said Aunt Mabel, "I broke the spout two years ago." His doubts resolved the Colonel temporized. "Fetch in Exhibits Two and Three," he ordered. The constables obediently retired and reappeared as if by magic with two battered and broken kitchen chairs. Aunt Mabel recognized these articles without undue difficulty.

During the next half-hour many and varied were the exhibits displayed before the court. The mists of the passing years have clouded the scene somewhat but I recall a beaten-up card table, a worn-out flashlight, a golden-oak rocker with embossed leather seat, a German silver bowl, an airtight heater (paper-thin from rust), cups and saucers, plates and bowls of heavy kitchen crockery (all entered as separate exhibits), and a bundle of ancient curtains despoiled by mouse, moth, and mildew.

When curtly asked by the magistrate to identify the latter, Aunt Mabel paused significantly and croaked, "If you were to ask me, I'd call them a bundle of old rags."

Not amused by her attitude of levity, Col. Dawson cleared his throat irritably whereupon Aunt Mabel became more attentive and positively identified her sister's drapes. Through all this procedure I had been a silent witness and soon Aunt Mabel and I were dismissed, and thanked for our cooperation.

During the tense scenes Fredric B. had stood furtively in his corner, his shifty eyes darting from face to face, his dirty fingers nervously twitching at his face and clothes. We had returned to the car and I was about to step in when Bardswell appeared at the courthouse door and asked me to return. Fearful of having in some way fallen afoul of the law, I hurried back and in a remarkably short time had vowed unswerving truth, had appeared to kiss the bible, and had positively identified the cheap and rusty nutcrackers that I had seen in happier days at Aunt Doll's, but which through some oversight, had not been exhibited for the benefit of Aunt Mabel. This done, I returned to the car and the bright, gusty March afternoon.

With much shared merriment Aunt Mabel and I drove homeward, but before turning in at our drive she asked as a favour if she might see the old log house where Aunt Doll had lived for so many years. We drove on till we reached the narrow winding trail beside the river and climbed slowly up to the railway track then on up again through the thick growth of broom and brambles to Aunt Doll's long neglected garden. A few timid snowdrops peeped beneath the tangled wreckage of shrub and tattered perennial, but desolation was evident despite the sunshine and blue sky. Aunt Mabel and I entered the lonely old cabin which had seen so much of mirth and laughter in happier days.

Fredric B. and others of his kind had taken everything that could be moved. They had left behind a loneliness, a taint on the air, an eeriness that could not be dispelled. Aunt Mabel and I were glad to return to the car and back to my parent's home for supper. Later I drove Aunt Mabel back to Duncan where she caught a bus for Victoria. Fredric B. was, I believe, sentenced to a jail term of six months hard labor at Okalla Prison Farm and I have never heard of him since. These, as I believe, are the true facts concerning the case of Rex versus Frederic B.

Edit. Note: The author uses some fictitious names in this story.

CHAPTER FIVE

Poems

Along with his delightful stories, Trevor Green also penned a number of poems. Here is a selection.

Elegy for a Frog

Hard by the railway-track there dwelt
An ancient frog, with horny pelt;
His world was centered in the pond,
The shore, and sloping bank beyond.
For years untold, his life had been
Moral, exemplary, serene.
In winter chill, he slept contented
Beneath the ice, in mud cemented.
In spring, his voice was soonest heard
Proclaiming loud the cheery word,
That days of snow and cold were gone,
That winter perished, pale and wan,
That breezes warm, and perfume-laden
Saluted spring (that fickle maiden!)

And later, with an air serene,
With lady-frog, bedecked in green
He'd swim in state around the shore,
Followed by pollywogs galore!
But, on a late November day,
Lured by the sun's departing ray,
He longed to bask upon the shore,
To feel the friendly warmth once more.
Before preparing to depart,
He sought the lady of his heart,
Conveyed to her his bold intention,
Bade her farewell with condescension:
With bulging eyes, and aching back,
He struggled upward to the track.
How steep the bank! How rough the gravel!
The matted grass delayed his travel.
How pale the sun! How chill the air!
But, near the goal, he did not care.
At last the summit he had gained,
With heart a-flutter, muscles strained.
Nor did he hear, as on he blundered,
The distant train's approaching thunder.
For him, no bell, no whistle sounded,
As when upon the rail he bounded!
A sickening "CRUNCH" and all was over.
His head lay severed in the clover!
His legs performed a wild gyration
The train swept onward to the station!
At dusk, a widowed lady-frog,
Her vigil kept upon a log;
The night wind blew, the cold stars glimmered,
While in her heart resentment simmered.
(Until restored to faith sublimer,
She thought her mate a bold two-timer!)

When came the dawn, and he came not,
She sought at last the fatal spot;
And found, O tragic evidence—
Her Master's soul departed hence!
She, mute with grief, and wild abandon,
Essayed herself the Rail to stand on.
(She could not know, until the Monday,
No Train would come, for this was Sunday!)
At last, oppressed by mortal anguish,
She reached the pond, wherein to languish;
To seek the mud, alone to mourn,
To curse the day that she was born!
Now months have passed, and skies are fairer,
Birds sing the praise of Primavera;
And it may pass that You, O friend,
Should near the pond your footsteps wend.
Then mark, all ye, when passing by,
The widow's moan, the orphan's cry!
Posthumous tadpoles, clad in black,
With woeful air swim past the track!
If you, in mood inclined to pity,
Should ask the moral of this ditty,
I cannot say; it might be this'n:
BE CAREFUL! STOP, LOOK, AND LISTEN!"

Green Mirror

Green Mirror, lushly framed in gold
Of buttercups that fringe the edge,
The restless breezes passing by
Sing secrets to the whispering sedge.
Wild roses, leaning from the bank
Shed scented tears that downward float

To meet the wave, and sail away—
Each one a crumpled petal-boat;
And willow boughs of silver-gray,
Like fairy wands in ancient lore,
In graceful pattern weave and sway
In praise of this enchanted shore.
A flashing wing, a liquid note
From joyous birds that swiftly pass;
The dragonfly's enameled coat
Glints blue above the meadow grass;
Then, when the cloak of night is drawn
And skies are strewn with cloudy bars
The peace of God transcending all,
Dark mirror, dusted faint with stars.

Lines on Presenting a jar of Honey to some Valued Friends, Xmas 1944

Don't look a gift horse in the mouth,
(An adage old, but true.)
Despise not then this humble gift,
That I present to you.
Think of the labour of the bees,
The ceaseless toil that wrought it!
Think of the stings of T. S. G.
(Defying hell he sought it.)
J.P. will find, (unto his cost!)
My gift, though sweet, is sticky;
And to consume it, *comme il faut*,
Requires a technique tricky!
Sweets to the sweet, Fair Allison!
(Thou housewife tried and true!)
There's none to be compared to thee

At Camp Six, or Youbou!
"Out of the eater came forth meat."
(Whence, Pat, these words and meaning?)
Pursue thy learning endlessly,
Fresh truth forever gleaning.
Bill Shakespeare and his Anne, (they say,)
Had bloody awful rows!
(By this I do not mean that you
Should clean up on your spouse!)
Despite the facts of history,
Which gloss such details o'er,
Henry the Sixth, it seems, was penned
The night he broke her jaw.
So, Pat, in spite of outward odds,
Exploit your talents latent,
Invoke the muse, and thrill the world
With prose and poems blatant!
You could not pen a lusty rhyme
With errors more than THIS has,
I thus conclude, but wish you ALL,
A VERY MERRY CHRISTMAS!

Gala Day at the elegant Lakeside Hotel in Lake Cowichan brings everyone out in their Sunday best.

The Legend of the Indian Paintbrush

By the shores of Lake Cowichan, by the lofty Mount Mesachie,
In a cavern on the mountain, in a dark and rocky cavern
Dwelt the chieftain, hidden ruler, dwelt the mighty mountain spirit.
In his hands he held the thunder, in his eyes there flashed the lightning,
From his lips the rains descended; when he sighed, the forests shuddered;
In his footsteps flowers blossomed, when he spoke, the hills resounded.

All the native tribes together yearly came to pay him homage,
Yearly came to do him honour, and he kindly smiled upon them
And he blessed them and their children; when he counselled, they
obeyed him
And their enemies they vanquished and they dwelt in peace together,
Harmony and joy created near the Cowichan's sparkling waters,
In the shade of Mount Mesachie.

Once, there strayed upon the shingle long ago, a radiant vision;
Black her hair as raven's plumage, white her skin as frost at midnight,
Red her lips as scarlet poppies, slim her form as silver birches;
Loveliest of all the Bradys, handsomer than all the Rosses,
Than the Todds and the MacConnels, than the Wilsons and the Williams,
Fairer far than all the Frickers, than the Millers and the Butcharts.

Lovelier than all around her, but, her fingernails were loathsome.
Long they were, and sharply pointed like the claws of turkey buzzards,
Like the teeth of alligators and she painted them vermilion.
And she would not heed the counsel of her friends who would advise her,
Of her mother when she murmured, "Trim thy nails, my best beloved!"
Of her daughter when she simpered, "Do not paint thy nails, O Mother!"

Of her son when he besought her, "Cut thy nails, I do implore thee!"
Of her spouse when he commanded, "Cut thy nails and do so quickly!"
Would not listen to their warnings, mocked and scorned their admonitions.

And the summer days grew shorter and her fingernails grew longer.
Thus, in all her matchless beauty she appeared upon the lakeshore,
Robed herself in scanty raiment, floated lightly on the waters,
Cleaved the waves like seaborne mermaid, floated like a lotus blossom,
Smiled upon the world before her, smiled upon her friends about her,
Spread her happiness around her.

High upon the nearby summit watched the mighty mountain spirit:
Calm and tranquil his reflections, calm as waters limned in moonlight;
Tranquil as the mists of autumn, holy was his meditation;
Holy was his inner conscience. From his seat upon the mountain
Spied he then the lovely creature, saw her gambol in the waters,
Heard her peals of carefree laughter; spellbound, he beheld her beauty,

Saw her loveliness before him, charmed by all her radiant glory,
Till at last he glimpsed her fingers, saw the long and scarlet talons;
Frowned he then in disapproval, summoned, in his wrath, an eagle,
Counselled it to bear a message to the fair but wayward damsel,
To acquaint her with her folly, that she might repent her actions.
Circling near, the mighty eagle to the maid revealed the warning

From the just but stern great spirit, how he scorned the meretricious,
How he scorned all false adornments, how he shunned all gaudy trappings,
How he ordered her to trim them, trim the long and flaming talons,
Never more to paint them scarlet, never more to let them flourish
More than nature had intended. Heard the mighty master's order,
With a firm and bold demeanour thus she turned to face the eagle

To convey her ultimatum, "Honored lord, I hear thy counsel,
In all else do I obey thee, I obey thy every bidding,
But my nails are mine to deal with if they grow as long as yardsticks,
If I paint them red as fire, they are mine, and I will keep them
And I will not heed thy warning!" Back across the shining waters
To the lofty mountain summit, soared the eagle heavy laden,

Laden with his woeful tidings. Well he knew that ill portended
When the master's will was flouted. Grieved he for the foolish creature,
Knowing well that danger threatened those who scorned the greatest spirit,
Those who would not keep his counsel, those who mocked and jeered at virtue.
Then, from out the smiling heavens stole a thread of misty vapor,
Stole a cloud of wintry aspect, moaned the wind among the rushes,

Sighed among the willow bushes, tossed the waves upon the shingle,
Splashed and fretted on the pebbles, dark and stormy grew the waters,
Fled the birds away for safety while the foolish, wayward woman
Sped across the shore in terror, sought concealment in the forest,
Sought to hide from the great spirit, sought to quell her guilty conscience
On her knees in supplication made an offer of atonement,

Offered up a prayer for mercy; but in vain was her contrition,
Fruitless her remorse and terror, for, within the darkening forest,
Louder than the roaring tempest, fiercer than the lightning flashes,
Came the tread of this high ruler, came the thunder of his breathing,
Came his shouts of rage and anger, came his screams and threats of vengeance,
Blazed his eyes with wrath and passion, stamped he there amid the mosses,

Wrenched the trees and tore their branches, glared among the rocks and grasses;
Peered between the stumps and bushes; could not find the hapless creature,
Could not hear her tortured breathing, could not hear her squeaks for mercy,
Could not see her, crouched in terror underneath the fronds of bracken,
With her black hair drawn about her that her white skin would not glimmer,
Would not glimmer in the darkness, in the black and gloomy forest.

When, at last, the mighty spirit, weary from his fruitless searching,
Still consumed with rage and fury, turned once more to gaze about him,
Peered in silence through the darkness, looked again about the forest,
Saw a gleam of brilliant scarlet move beneath a leaf of bracken,
Saw the long and painted fingers, heard them as they clicked together.
Clicked and rattled as they trembled, saw them glow like coals of fire,

Saw them curl in supplication. With a scream of vicious anger
Flung himself upon the woman: deaf to all her shrieks for pardon,
Crushed the breath of life within her, pounded her into a jelly,
Tore the nails from off her fingers, ripped her hair in savage fury,
Stamped upon her broken body, ground her fragile bones to powder.
Never more was seen the maiden, never more beside the waters,

Never more within the forests, never was a trace discovered
Of the spot where she had perished, where the mountain god had
found her.
Yet, there grows upon the hillside, thrives beside the rippling water,
Grows a plant of tender beauty; leafless from the soil it springeth,
Frail its stalk, though dark and slender; for its crown it bears a halo
Bears a plume of scarlet petals, each as red as sparks of fire,

Each as bright as deepest crimson: learned men name it "Castilleia",
Guileless children call it "Paint Brush", stupid folk say, "Them is poppies":
Only those who know the legend rightly term it "Ann-Lees's Fingers",
Call it by its truthful symbol.
Might it be that the great spirit in his wisdom, moved to pity,
When the foolish woman mocked him, in his mercy made this flower

That her fellow-man might profit as a warning of her folly,
As a tribute to her beauty? Others have a different version.
"This," they say, "is Ann-Lee's Fingers; see it grow beside the forest,
See it flourish in the meadows, how it thrives upon the mountain;
Still in death she mocks the master, waves her hands in sheer defiance,
Flaunts her scarlet fingers boldly, taunts and scoffs at the great ruler."

The mountains of the Cowichan Valley were a magnet to Trevor Green, who loved hiking the Island's forests.

Delayed Salute to Adeline, a Flood Victim

(Allan and Adeline Anderson lived on a riverside property downstream from Greendale)

When the waters higher swirled,
And made a shambles of your world
Did you, as you paced the floor
Sympathize with Father Noah?
Though, by time and space divided
Respective problems coincided.
(He, perplexed by God's decree
To build an ark, and put to sea;
You were similarly troubled
As the river surged and bubbled.)
Did you stop to contemplate

What Ham and Shem and Japheth ate?
Or, were you privately concerned
To see which way the current turned?
Mrs. Noah, perchance, was puzzled
How best to keep the lions muzzled.
You, a thousand aeons later,
Were immersed in household data:
If the waters in should seep,
Where to go, and what to keep?
Should you leave the rugs and such
To the rivers's clammy touch?
Should the radio be lifted
And the chairs and tables shifted?
How to raise the grand piano?
What to do with Roy's Meccano?
How to cook without a fire?
How to keep the sawdust drier?
(Questions such as these arise
When disaster rules our lives)
In the life beyond the veil
Should celestial pleasures fail
You may find, a friend sincere
Mrs. Noah will lend an ear.
You and she may chat with mirth
Of when the waters ruled on earth.
Of how you kept the children dry,
Of how she coaxed the dove to fly.
(Friendship thrives on topics fitting,
Floods, canasta, bridge and knitting.)
Over cups of milk and mead
Past calamities recede
While, beneath Elysian sky
Noah and Allan wander by;

Each in earnest conversation
Mainly about navigation.
How one made the ark to float,
How the other built his boat.
(Topics such as these discuss:
Copper nails will NEVER rust;
Which material is cheaper:
Gopher wood or yellow cedar?)
Then, as evening closes in,
Allan plays his violin;
While, in a contralto choice
Japheth's wife will lift her voice;
As her clear tones higher soar,
You will wish you'd practised more
You, whose voice could reach perfection
Will be plunged in deep dejection
What a strange, triangular life!
Allan, you, and Japheth's wife!
That this scandal should not be
Practise scales unceasingly
Notes staccato, coloratura
Ever clearer, ever surer!
Think what triumphs lie before
TV, broadcasts, concert tour,
Handsome contracts, glowing press,
But chiefly, Allan's happiness.
And to be hailed, in church or pub
FIRST LADY OF THE MUSIC CLUB!

Tree #19

The vigilance of those that stand beside
Thy twisted form, in this enchanted glade,
Conceals from view, and seeks in vain to hide
What God in His omnipotence has made.
If, in this tortured shape, perchance there dwell
A human soul, condemned to thus endure,
What crime in ages past did he compel
Till years of restitution make him pure?
If destiny, unaided, were to trace
Thy future span upon the sands of time,
How soon might scourge or tempest thee erase,
And leave, once more, this shadowed glen sublime
But ah, the hand of man has interceded
Thy progeny shall flourish, unimpeded.

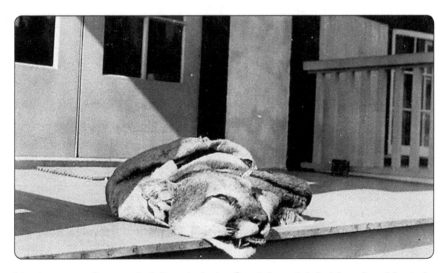

Hunters were frequent visitors to Lake Cowichan, joining local residents in the forests in search of the abundant game animals, such as this cougar.

Other Stories by Trevor Green

Unique Features in Cowichan Lake

*I*n order to complete my account of the various islands in the lake, I feel I should include excerpts from an article written 54 years ago by the Rev. Robert Connell, a regular correspondent to the *Victoria Daily Times*. He lived at Sooke I believe, and in addition to his position in the church there, he was a keen student of nature and a most observant man.

He had been invited to pay a visit to the forestry station at Mesachie Lake, which had been in operation for three years, and he describes in detail the trip by car from Victoria and the winding dusty road from Duncan to the Lake. Before reaching the forestry station, he first paid a visit to the Simpson and Stoker gardens after which the forestry boat took him across the lake to the camp. The afternoon and evening were spent in exploring the station, such as it was, in 1932, and he expresses a keen interest in the several experiments in thinning and fertilizing that he saw.

From here on, I quote directly from his text, written on June 10, 1932.

"I shall now take my readers to an altogether different scene and object of investigation. After our evening meal on the first day we started out for a point about halfway between the extremities of the lake on the south side. Under the dark and lofty pass of Bald Mountain, we ran past Goat Island and through the narrows separating it from the main body of water.

Our destination was marked by a small island with outlying reefs of rock beyond which a little creek with a boat-house appears on a place of low-lying swampy ground. Here we went ashore to find ourselves on a series of bare ribs of rock running out into the lake. Curiously harsh in texture to the hand and dotted with clumps of plants, these ribs are a portion of the underlying rocks of the valley basin which here break through the inner rim of cretaceous sediments. While the latter have their strike, or lengthways direction, or run of their beds parallel to the shore of the lake, these older rocks here cut across that strike almost at right angles and pass out thus under the water.

I had long been hoping to see this very exposure, which Clapp describes in his memoir on southern Vancouver Island and which has a great interest to geologists as being one of the definite time-markers in the Island's geological history. Further, it provides in a somewhat spectacular way a proof of the theory that the original condition of the present Island was a volcanic archipelago with associated coral reefs. It was the opportunity of seeing for myself these reef-building corals that made this expedition for me more exciting than perhaps either of my companions guessed.

We lost no time in beginning our search for the evening was fast falling. Soon we found what we sought and it was far more thrilling than I had anticipated, for Clapp is a singularly cool and restrained writer. Here were long masses of reed-leaf coral; there, grouped clusters of smaller star-like species occur. Altogether five distinct species of corals from this locality were identified some years ago by Dr. Shimer, the well-known American paleontologist. In addition there are quantities of consolidated fragments of shell and coral, while in places very perfect specimens of shells are found, both bivalves and univalves, some of them marked by rather ornate sculpture. In one narrow bed there is a considerable amount of carbonaceous matter, which may represent either plant or animal life."

Robert Connell then goes on to describe the corals of the Great Barrier Reef in Australia, and conjectures about the similarity between them and what he has found on the small island in the lake. He continues thus:

"What were the conditions under which these reef-building corals lived in this latitude far north of the most northerly occurrences of today? Reef-building corals require, it is agreed, for their development clean shallow water with a temperature at the surface of at least 68 degrees F. Thus they are found everywhere between 30 degrees north and the same distance south of the equator, except on the western shores of the continents where they are exposed to upwelling cold water, the result of prevalent off-land winds. Thus they are absent from the west coast[s] of South Africa and South America in spite of the tropical temperatures.

It would appear, then, that when these reef-building corals of Vancouver Island flourished, the temperature of the sea was not only many degrees warmer, but that the whole condition of things must have been altogether other than it is today. Our knowledge of the earth's surface in those days, imperfect as it is, gives us the key to the mystery. But first the interesting fact is to be noted that the eight species of fossils identified from this ancient reef are found to have curious affinities geographically. Thus three of them find their nearest kin in Central Europe; two in England; one in England and India; one in England, India, and Europe; and one in Europe and California. None have affinities with fossils from the eastern side of the continent, where the Triassic and Jurassic rocks are almost wholly of fresh-water origin.

The testimony of the rocks is that in Triassic and Jurassic times, the Pacific Ocean, then united with the ancient Mediterranean sea which extended across India and northern Africa and by a northern extension to the British Isles, flooded as a shallow continental sea the western coast of America, reaching east of the present Rocky Mountain area and almost meeting the waters of the south which flooded Central America. West of where Vancouver Island now is was a continental mass, now vanished in the depths of the Pacific. Dana pointed out long ago that there was in the Jurassic a 'remarkable uniformity of climate over the globe,' and that even the 'climate of the Arctic regions was then probably at least warm-temperate.' He goes on to say that 'the whole ocean was warm enough for the heat required for coral to be borne as far as northern England.'

The Jurassic period in this part of the world was marked by a very great outbreak of submarine volcanic activity, both explosions and outflows of lava being registered in the rocks. They occur throughout the whole length and breadth of Vancouver Island, broken, of course, by later intrusions and superficially by the later sediments. Earth movements in the late Jurassic led to folding of these volcanic rocks, and thus the reefs on Cowichan Lake are tipped towards the northwest at rather steep angle. This folding on a gigantic scale produced the beginnings of the Sierra Nevada, Cascade and Coast Ranges, while the Coast Range of California with the Klamath and other mountain ranges were probably extended out to sea in the land mass to the west of Vancouver Island and the Queen Charlotte group.

From the reef we returned to the little island close at hand; it is composed of a black vesicular lava, that is, one filled with steam cavities. In the growing dusk it was impossible to examine the whole circumference, but I believe the reefs off-shore and lying just above the water at the present height of the lake are coral ones, accessible at the low level of summer water."

This, then, is the summary of one who was well-informed on the subject of geology, and who wrote in great detail of his findings many years ago. While at present the level of the lake is at least a constant three feet higher since the weir was completed, and the reefs referred to by Robert Connell are now doubtless submerged, it might be a worthwhile project for some of our scuba divers to make a survey and to reveal their discoveries to the press.

Years ago, when the road was constructed to Caycuse from Honeymoon Bay, in a certain rock cut on the left hand side, away from the shore, I have found several fossils of shells, clearly imprinted in the sandstone, bearing out the statement of Robert Connell.

The Jurassic period dates back over 200 million years and one is tempted to wonder what contemporary fossils will be found and by whom even a half-million years from now. I find it of much interest to learn that here, in our quiet backwater of the Island, we have the geological testament of prehistoric times.

[Editor's note: We may see new interest in these rock formations now as changes in climate, the lake level, and the Lake Cowichan weir may expose these unique features again, making them available for study.]

Back in the pre-weir days, McCallum's Bridge had been a way to get from the south side of Lake Cowichan to North Shore Road.

A bit more about the Islands

O n the wall of our kitchen there hangs a large map of the Cowichan Lake area. It depicts clearly the lake, the surrounding mountain ranges, as well as the many creeks and water systems that enter it. The islands, too, stand out clearly, and are numbered from one to 10, from east to west. There is a theory that originally the lake drained to the west into the system of the Nitinat River and thus out to the Pacific Ocean, and it may well have been so. Some years ago, when successive winter flooding resulted in severe damage to the Duncan area, there was speculation over gouging out a deep trench into the Nitinat Valley to relieve pressure on the Cowichan River. But because of the prohibitive costs involved this plan was abandoned.

The first of the islands is close to the south shore at Lakeview Park. It is virtually unchanged in appearance from snapshots taken in the early 1900s, when early logging was active in that area. The second island is a small cluster of willow brush as one approaches Marble Bay, far too impenetrable and low-lying to consider as an overnight campsite. But Goat Island, number three is far larger and now supports a fine forest of conifers and alder, replacing the original growth that was destroyed by fire many decades ago. I believe that on this island the late Dr. Stoker kept his goats, so that they might not destroy the fine garden that had been developed at his property, which is now owned by the University of Victoria.

The next island, confusingly enough, is also known as Goat Island, and lies a short distance off North Shore Road as one approaches Youbou. It, too, is quite unspoiled and adds greatly to the fine views from this point.

I retain vivid memories of the fifth island, lying farther west, and near the south shore, for one fine July day in 1919 a party of perhaps a dozen parents and children had hired a launch to take them through the narrows and into the big lake for a picnic. This was relatively unknown country to many visitors to the lake more than 65 years ago and few of the adults were aware of how suddenly the winds can spring up on a hot summer afternoon in this area. It was impossible to land in the narrows, so our guide steered for the nearest island through mountainous waves. Anxious parents urged terrified children to sit on the bottom of the boat, and it was suggested that we should pray and pray we did and it was a great relief when we landed safely at the island.

But delightful as this brief interlude may have been, hanging over us all was the knowledge and the dread of the return journey, for the wind had not lessened and the waves, if anything seemed even higher. Nor was it of much comfort to learn that there were no life-jackets in the boat; they were seldom available anyway in those days.

But what with prayers and the expertise of our guide, we came safely through the narrows and into the lower lake where the wind had lessened. And an added thrill, as we neared "the Foot", was to see the Empire Lumber Company's loading wharf ablaze, flames leaning skyward in the wind, and houseboat dwellers casting off their mooring lines to escape from the inferno.

Island number six lies close to the south shore, and is clearly visible from the Caycuse campsite. It, too, seems to be quite unspoiled without trace of fires or vandalism. Farther to the west lie numbers seven, eight, and nine, grouped closely together, presenting a most pleasing view to the east from Caycuse. I have not, as yet, visited these islands but they are doubtless familiar picnic spots for boaters and campers.

Last of all comes Deadman's Island, number 10, lying close to the south shore. The name results from a sinister discovery in the early 1920s when two hunters, marooned overnight due to a severe storm, sought shelter in a sort of grotto formed by overhanging rocks. Here they discovered several small cedar bark boxes containing the bones of children. It is believed that these children had perished in the smallpox epidemic that had decimated the native tribes on the west coast at that time, and as a safety precaution, the small victims in the cedar bark coffins had been left in the cave rather than risk the spread of infection by removing them to the cemetery at Duncan.

Subsequently they were interred in the Indian graveyard.

Years later, my wife and I spent a night on Deadman's Island. We found the grotto, and, what we believed to be one or two fragile pieces of rib cage, though they could equally well have been scraps of small cedar limbs, free of bark.

Each of the islands of Cowichan Lake has its individual beauty and each is worth a visit.

The Old Ashburnham Barn

Campers and visitors returning to the Gordon Bay campsite after some years away will notice with surprise and dismay the desolation resulting from the recent logging between Robertson River and Honeymoon Bay. Some will say with approval, "Oh, now you can see the lake," whereas others will lament the destruction of the beautiful second-growth forest that provided a fitting approach to Ashburnham's Beach, a forest that surely was worth inclusion in a list of tourist attractions.

Those driving slowly past may notice the sagging structure of what is generally known as Ashburnham's Barn, the history of which is worthy of review.

Around the years 1887-1888, a number of settlers moved into the area, one of whom was Charles Bailey, originally from Ireland. He acquired acreage on the lakeshore, in the vicinity of Ashburnham's Beach, and cleared land in order to provide space for a two-storey house, built of logs, and a fine large barn. I believe that this property had been previously logged, the timber being hauled by horses or oxen to the lakeshore and later floated down the river to Cowichan Bay.

Charles Bailey was not, I understand, a remittance man. He undoubtedly possessed capital to develop his property and to concentrate on raising beef cattle for market. Every second year most of his stock was herded down to the foot of the lake by a rough trail through the forest and forded across the river at a shallow spot near the Nickerson property. The late Charles March and his elder brother assisted with the cattle drive, which took about three days before reaching Duncan where the cattle auction was held.

Land was cleared around the house and barn for pasture and an orchard was established of which a few fruit trees remain. During the early 1900s, due to ill health, Charles Bailey sold his property to a Victoria real-estate firm and returned to his native Ireland. In 1913, part of the estate was purchased by the Lawrence Ashburnham family, who built a fine house close to the lake.

Farther to the west was the B. G. Archibald property, later to become the Western Forest Industries guesthouse.

The Ashburnhams had the use of the old log barn for their saddle ponies and for storing hay but the Bailey house was vacant for some time.

In late 1933, the firm of McDonald and Murphy sold their logging interests west of Honeymoon Bay to Hunter and Rounds to form the Lake Logging Company, and at the same time the Ashburnham and Bailey properties were purchased.

The Ralph Rounds family hailed from Wichita, Kansas, and in the summer of 1934 arrived to occupy the Ashburnham floathouse, after having spent an interval at the Riverside Hotel and at Greendale.

The ménage included Mrs. Ralph Rounds, her two sons, a chauffeur, and a secretary.

Extensive plans were proposed for the Bailey property. The log barn was to become a sort of gymnasium and the house to be occupied by a resident caretaker. A new cedar shake roof for the barn was completed that year but the Rounds family did not return to the lake thereafter. The old house was destroyed by fire, the usual fate of old buildings located far from the village, and the floathouse was rented from time to time until its final re-location on shore at Honeymoon Bay.

Later, Western Forest Industries established a most attractive picnic site at Ashburnham's Beach. Benches and tables and facilities were provided, but it is a sorry reflection on present-day trends to note that the wanton destruction of the picnic site was the work of vandals. Broken glass, shattered tables, and fire-pits testify to their efforts.

And now, with the splendid forest a shambles since the logging, there seems little to attract the visitor to Ashburnham's Beach. We are fortunate, indeed, to have in our midst such fine artists as Gaylia Nelson, Carol Rettig and others, who have painted pictures of the old barn.

At one point some years previously there was a suggestion that as a historical building it might be dismantled and brought down piece by piece and log by log to become a local museum. But the deterioration of many of the logs and the roof made such plans impractical.

It remains, then, for the forces of wind and weather, of heavy snows or incendiarism by vandals to write "finis" to the old log barn, when "the place thereof will know it no more."

The Swimming Party

*W*hen the big blue Cadillac sedan made the sharp turn from Esquimalt Road into Head Street and lumbered down the long hill towards the seaside estate of Brigadier-General and Mrs. Sutherland Brown, my apprehensions were greatly augmented.

In the back of the car, Miss Betty Ward, surrounded by boxes, bags, garments, and trunks of every description, chatted, with laboured pleasantry to Aunt Lillian, who was intent on the serious problem of getting the Cadillac safely to the lower levels, without driving into the ditch. Myfanwy, seated between Aunt Lillian and me, also kept up a merry flow of chatter, the while regarding her silk-clad legs with marked approval.

But here was I, invited to a very select swimming party, never having met host or hostess, and feeling sure I wouldn't know a soul among the merry throng. Myfawny had reassured me slightly by saying that she and I would in all probability be the oldest guests present, but even then I felt very nervous when I pictured myself playing water-tag with a crowd of little toddlers, and blowing up little junior's water wings. Then I imagined that after the swimming we might have to dance and then I'd have to dance with the hostess; I had a vision of the Brigadier in a fit of jealousy menacing me with his old army revolver. So my thoughts sped on.

There wasn't much time for reflection, however, for by now we had reached the foot of the hill towards the barracks. Aunt Lillian dexterously guided the Cadillac's straying wheels along the wide road. Around a sharp corner, and we saw in front a warlike fence of barbed wire, painted white and with spear-like arrangements atop every post, enclosing green lawns. In the distance the erect figure of a sentry strode along beside the fence. Under the hot August sun I felt for the moment as though I'd gladly exchange places with him.

By now we had entered the great iron gates, which had fearsome looking cannon beside each post. A second sentry, the replica of the first, peered at us out of his little sentry-box as we drove through. Betty busied herself in collecting her various possessions. The road now wound past tall white-painted buildings of an austere appearance, making sharp turns around blind corners. Glimpses of the sea were visible between the buildings. A final sharp turn south brought us to the end of the road, which circled neatly around a small grass plot, like a tiny green island that harbored a single oak tree. The Cadillac halted thankfully. I got out, followed by Myfanwy, and opened the rear door to help Betty to alight but my eyes were rewarded by the sight of her back disappearing through the other door. A menial of refined appearance, clad in blue serge trousers and starched white frock-coat, now bustled up with dignified haste, the sun gleaming on his bald head and scrubby white moustache. He took Miss Ward's suitcase, and disappeared into the house. Aunt Lillian, Myfanwy, Betty, and I walked around to the front.

It was a really charming spot. The house, a long, high, narrow, and very formal home was like the other buildings, painted white. A long verandah sloped away to a green lawn in front, surrounded by riotous flowerbeds and shrubbery. Beyond that lay the sea. There was no sign of the swimming-pool. Part of the lawn was decorated by tables, chairs, rugs, and cushions. Several smartly dressed ladies wandered aimlessly about, and here and there a harassed-looking servitor scuttled. A tall lady in white detached herself from a distant group and strode across the lawn to where we stood on the path below the verandah. "Hello Lillian dear," cried the lady, as she neared us, "So glad you came." Then Aunt Lillian said, "This is Mrs. Brown." We were introduced with all due ceremony.

A word now about my general impressions of Mrs. Sutherland Brown. A white knitted silk sweater with a blue border, and a white silk pleated skirt accentuated the lines of her figure. Her bony silk clad legs terminated in large feet which were crammed into small, white, expensive-looking shoes. A large, brimless hat, (white, to match the general scheme), shaped exactly like one of those covers, made of fine wire-netting, which are placed over meat to keep the flies away, covered almost her whole head, so that when one saw her back view, no neck was visible. Through the red gash of her painted lips, false teeth gleamed. The rest of her face was a white mask of powder, through which her jade green eyes glittered. Black carved earrings swung from her ears.

After a few conventional remarks, Mrs. Brown asked, "Trevor, you brought your bathing suit, didn't you." To my affirmative, she continued, "Do you see that little hut over there?" Here she pointed, jewels flashing on her manicured fingers. "Well, that's the boys' dressing room and just come back here when you're ready, the Brigadier will show you the way to the pool." With that, she, Aunt Lillian, Betty, and Myfanwy made off in the general direction of the backs of a group of women, who were seated on a rug overlooking the swimmers. The white skirt swung from Mrs. Brown's hips with each step in the true hula girl manner.

I hurried over to the Cadillac, got my bathing-suit and towel, and proceeded towards the little white hut that my hostess had indicated. It was behind and to the left of the main house and a short distance from the driveway. I entered the hut and closed the door. As is usual with most dressing rooms, the door refused to stay shut, for the lock was broken, so I propped someone's shoe against it with satisfactory results. Within, disorder and chaos reigned. Shoes and stockings, collars and ties, shirts, and trousers, jumbled together with coats and underwear, lay in untidy mounds upon the floor. The little room boasted one large and dirty window, which commanded a general view of the rear quarters of the house. I cleared a space among the garments on the floor to place my clothes. I slipped into my bathing suit, a sun-backed affair of two brilliant shades of blue, cached my watch in my coat pocket, and parked my glasses upon a nearby shelf. Then a thought struck me. Should I wear my shoes to go to the pool, or should I leave them here, and was it the correct thing to take my towel along? I didn't want it to look as though I'd never been to a swimming party before. After some cogitation, I resolved to leave both shoes and towel behind and slipped out of the hut.

I walked across the lawn to a group of backs among which I recognized Aunt Lillian's smart sports suit, and Myfanwy's green and white ensemble. They were chatting to Mrs. Brown, who stood with one hip stuck out in an attitude of defiance. She turned at my unheralded approach and surveyed me critically. Failing to observe any defects, she said, "Well Trevor, you didn't take long; I expect you'll find the water feels fine. Here's the Brigadier." A bulky figure toiled up the slope to where we stood. "Sonny," said Mrs. Brown, "this is Trevor Green, Lillian Spencer's cousin." I gave the Brigadier the once over. His dark brown hair was interspersed with gray and had receded into two small patches leaving a glistening reddish expanse, Sahara-like in its bareness. His small dark eyes peered from beneath thick tufts of unmanicured eyebrow. A long flowing moustache bearing a close resemblance to that of Sir Sidney in the Mutt and Jeff cartoons concealed the lower portion of his visage. A tight red bathing suit gave evidence of the extent to which his chest had slipped. We shook hands with the utmost friendliness. I had previously inquired of Myfanwy how one should address this celebrity, whether to call him Brigadier, or General, or Brigadier-General Brown and she had said, "I don't know for sure but I always call him Mr. Brown."

So, "Good afternoon, Mr. Brown," I said cordially, "I'm very pleased to make your acquaintance." The small eyes darted fire, and I realized my error at once. (Now I know all about addressing such personages). "Glad to know you," he replied angrily, "Quite a nice little pool we have here." After several further remarks concerning the advantages of the pool, he disappeared towards the house. "If you'd like to dive in first, Trevor," said Mrs. Brown, "there's a very good place just over here." I followed her to where the ladies sat. The rock over which the rugs were spread dropped away in a cliff-like formation, to the edge of the pool about 15 feet below. The pool resembled nothing so much as a slightly enlarged puddle in which a multitude of children splashed and shouted. It was separated from the sea by a low, narrow concrete wall, which connected a tiny rocky peninsula to the cliff below me.

Trevor Green enjoyed swimming all his life, taking to the Cowichan River in all weathers.

I pictured myself soaring down to the water surrounded by a crowd of frankly admiring toddlers in one of Mr. Craig's famous swallow dives and cleaving the water like a knife. But such a feat could be accomplished only in the imagination, because I can't do even an ordinary dive properly. So I thanked Mrs. Brown and explained that I'd rather go in the other way first and perhaps try a dive later. She then pointed out a little pathway on the left which led down to the pool to avoid the rock cliff, and repeating that the Brigadier would soon be along to show me over the pool, she departed to entertain some newly arrived guests.

Having reached the water's edge, I halted to survey the landscape. There were perhaps 30 or 40 young people, all enjoying themselves to the utmost. To the casual eye their ages ranged from two to 14 years. In the middle of the pool a small raft was stranded upon the bottom and here the children swarmed. The big idea of the moment was, it appeared, to tip the raft and it seemed hard that, despite the efforts of so many willing helpers, it refused to budge. Their heroic struggles caused the tepid water, so dirty that one could not see the bottom, to froth into hefty waves which splashed over the little concrete wall into the sea. I gazed for a time upon this spectacle and then entered the water.

After I had advanced half a dozen steps, the water was still midway between knee and ankle. This, apparently, was not the deep end. Avoiding the maelstrom about the raft, I swam across to the little wall, which I shall term the breakwater. During the process of making the first stroke I lacerated my chest, legs, elbows, arms and chin upon the barnacle covered rocks that formed the bottom. The second stroke found me in really deep water: about two feet deep! And halfway through the third stroke I had reached the breakwater, where I again lacerated my stomach upon a hidden boulder of large dimensions. Seated upon the narrow ridge of concrete I looked about me. Behind lay the ocean, so deep and cool and clean. In front lay a small, dirty puddle: the pool. On the left the rock cliff arose bearing aloft a delectable burden of ladies, intent on watching the swimmers.

Betty Ward caught my eye and favoured me with one of her slow, enigmatical smiles. Myfanwy looked longingly at the pool, wishing no doubt that she had refrained from eating so many meringues the previous night. (During the night watches she had been seized with a bilious attack).

Aunt Lillian, one shapely silk clad leg stretched in front of her while she sat on the other, conversed with Mrs. Russel Kerr, whose pretty painted face and piquant manner quite won the heart of little Campbell Sweeny (aged three), who from his vantage point upon the stranded raft, gazed up at her with pure devotion. Mrs. Brown lighted a cigarette in a jade holder, and took slow ruminative puffs, having difficulty in controlling her upper set of teeth while she made smoke rings. Through the bushes which screened the little path to the pool, I glimpsed the red bathing suit and paunchy rotundity of the Brigadier proceeding to the "shallow end," in order to see that all the guests were enjoying themselves.

Reasoning that he might not approve of my inactivity and apparent ennui, I slipped off the breakwater into the dirty depths and set out on a little expedition to explore the pool. I swam over to what was supposed to be the "deep end" directly below the cliff, where, had I followed my hostess' suggestion, I might have dived. Here the water was slightly less than four feet, which depth covered a spot perhaps three square feet in extent. Farther afield jagged barnacle-y rocks lay just below the surface. If I had dived, well, somebody else would be preparing sprouted oats for the chickens now. It is only charitable to suppose that Mrs. Brown was not familiar with the relative depths of the pool. It does her injustice to suppose that she was desirous of "finishing me off" after such a short acquaintance.

As I swam from the spot, nightmare visions arose. I pictured myself a lifeless corpse floating face downward on the surface, gore streaming from a jagged wound in my temple, the famous "Spencer nose" a bloody unrecognized mass. I pictured Mrs. Brown, swooning in her husband's arms, wailing, "Oh, Sonny, if I'd only known, if I'd only known." I saw Myfanwy, pale as death, and Aunt Lillian, paler still under her rouge, clasped in each other's arms. (Mine is an unusually vivid imagination).

But now a diversion arose. Children were still milling about the raft which hitherto had remained firmly fixed upon the bottom, confident of help which the Brigadier would proffer. Again it was the unexpected that happened. Brigadier-General Sutherland Brown was halfway to the raft when, amid roars of applause from the cliff, coupled with ecstatic shouts and cries of "Whoopee, whoopee" from the children, it suddenly floated free of the obstruction. Several toddlers, including little Campbell, were thrown off into the water, later reappearing to add to the tumult and shouting with sobs and lamentations. It was evident that the amount of water displaced by the nether portions of the Brigadier's body was more than sufficient to float the raft. Now they were able to tip the raft. "Whoopee," they cried in chorus at the prospect of such a thrill, and again, "Whoopee." But a sense of gratitude bade them await their benefactor, the Brigadier, so that he could be guest of honour at the tipping ceremony. He lurched up onto the raft, and lumbered up and down, his stomach quivering with the exertion. Children clambered beside him and rushed from one side to the other in wild abandon. The raft swayed and rocked, with increasing momentum; it creaked and cracked. The load of humanity caused it to submerge to the floor board, waves splashed against the cliff and over the breakwater. Excited nurses upon the beach wrung their hands in apprehension, and darted back and forth voicing warnings to their small charges, on or in the immediate vicinity of the raft. A splintering crack was the first intimation of the inevitable wreck. The raft lurched to one side, a shattered hulk. Children, screaming with excitement tumbled off into the angry storm-tossed waters. The Brigadier, losing his balance, disappeared amid the turmoil and for several seconds one fleshy heel was all that remained to mark the spot.

Thus the afternoon wore on and soon I was back again at the breakwater. The children still hung about the splintered raft, gazing at the ruins with fascination. I surveyed the crowd with complete boredom, when suddenly I glimpsed the skinny neck and green bathing suit of none other than "Pep" Pooley. I hurried over to where she stood knee deep in water. Not having seen her for more than a year, I was anxious to renew our old acquaintance. It was characteristic of her to express no surprise whatsoever at seeing me again, and after a few hasty comments concerning the weather and the attractions of the pool, she disappeared among the throng in search of Phyllis Parkes, her best friend, a girl of some 11 summers.

But now most of the bathers were leaving for Mrs. Brown had intimated that a delicious tea would be ready after the swim. Anxious not to appear too eager to quit the pool, I swam across to the shallow end, and after more painful injuries to arms and legs upon the shingle, I gained the shore. Here I encountered Miss Allen, who was employed in verbally preventing Campbell from going beyond his depth, not a difficult task. We engaged in conversation and exchanged many pleasant reminiscences concerning the happy summers which she and her young charges had spent at Greendale.

Soon all the bathers had left so, excusing myself, I hurried to the little dressing-room, now filled to capacity with members of the male sex all in various stages of undress. While we were dressing, someone on a tour of exploration came upon an old cutlass (presumably belonging to mine host) which lay concealed beneath a rotten board in the floor. This caused great excitement and it was doubtless due only to a dispensation of providence that someone was not stabbed. This discovery considerably prolonged the dressing interval. At last fully attired I left the hut in company with several other boys much younger than myself and after hanging our suits and towels upon a fence which bordered part of the drive, we approached the scene of festivity. While crossing the porch in the direction of the lawn we met Mrs. Brown, just coming out of the house. "Hello boys," she said, "I expect you're quite ready for tea now aren't you?" Highly embarrassed at being thus addressed, my companions forebore to reply, so I was obliged to make answer for the silent group. "Oh yes," I replied, "how very nice. I enjoyed the swim so much." This was untrue but Mrs. Brown seemed pleased. "Oh, I thought you would," she exclaimed, "It must be quite a nice change after bathing in a river all the time."

Now we had reached the lawn, where we stood around looking foolish. Rugs were spread about, and on these most of the female members of the party were seated. I caught sight of Myfanwy chatting with a freckle-faced girl whom she later introduced to me as Helen Douglas. Aunt Lillian had left in the Cadillac to make a round of social calls. Betty Ward was standing nearby making conversation with the Brigadier, who looked infinitely more presentable when fully dressed. Seated upon a pile of cushions, her slender legs crossed in front of her, Mrs. Russel Kerr was improving the shining hours by knitting away at a white baby jacket for her youngest born who, by reason of her tender years, was not present at the party. She paused to pull out a jeweled compact and after a brief scrutiny of her face in the little mirror, she proceeded to make repairs upon her lips. Not until they were thick with paint, and their outline quite visibly altered, did she snap the little case shut. Her mouth now resembled a streak of blood. Next bestowing little pats with a white hand, she tucked a straying curl of her tinted, bronze-y hair beneath her large picture hat. Feeling now at peace with the world, she caught up on her knitting.

It was whilst I was watching her with marked interest, for she was really quite pretty, that Mrs. Brown's strident tones broke in upon my reverie. "Sit down, boys," she said. "No, not on the grass, there's a rug just there." We complied with alacrity and fell to talking about school, and about the personalities of certain girls present. Preparations for tea now became apparent. An elderly lady of dignified mien approached with a tray-load of glasses, which she proffered to each child. A servitor approached from the house with a white enamel pitcher containing lemonade, which he poured with dexterity into the glasses. A pretty maid passed platefuls of buttered currant buns. For a long time, this appeared to be all on the menu. Mrs. Brown kept organizing little campaigns to prevent any of her guests from sitting on the lawn instead of on the rug.

Campbell Sweeny, who sat near us, was a picture of woe. He had ceased trying to bite his first bun, and was now gnawing a dried-up currant, making fretful and peevish remarks concerning the character of the food. His immediate neighbours strove to quiet him, but despite their efforts his mutterings grew louder and louder until they reached a clearly enunciated wail of, "Oh, I thought there'd be cake." Miss Allen effectually subdued her young charge, who was gladdened by the sight of the maid appearing from the house bearing two platters of chocolate-iced cake. At this juncture, a diversion arose. A large canary-coloured Studebaker 8 Sedan had crept noiselessly up the drive and had halted near the little grass plot. Mr. Russel Kerr alighted and Mrs. Brown now perceiving him cried, "Good boy, Russel. So you were able to come after all." Mr. Kerr neared the little group, where he was met by the Brigadier, who proffered refreshment. After a short conversation with his host, Russel turned towards his spouse, who was in difficulties with the baby-jacket and was seeking advice from an elderly lady of refined appearance, who seemed to be experienced in such matters. She turned at his approach. "Hello, Russ, old man," she said. "Had a hard day at the office? How about a swim?" Mrs. Brown, who happened to be passing by, overheard this last query. "No, he's coming in with me," she declared, linking a possessive arm through that of Mr. Kerr. "You will won't you, Russ old dear? Poor old man, you look so tired, a swim will buck you up like anything. Come on, let's go." Muttering an excuse to his wife, Russel turned and went into the house with the lady of his choice. Shortly after they reappeared, Mrs. Brown, clad in a black sun-back bathing suit over which she wore a black silk wrap, generously ornamented with designs of spiders and spiders webs done in silver. She wore black rubber bathing-shoes with large white rubber spiders on the toes. Her head, divested of the strange hat, was covered with short black hair, which showed a distinct line of gray down the parting. Russel was attired in a sun-back suit of two colours of red, which was far too small for him. Arm in arm, they went off to the pool the objects of the baleful glances of Mrs. Kerr.

During their absence, the ice-cream made its appearance. This was dispensed by the Brigadier, and was brought around by the servitor. More cake was handed round and several kinds of sandwiches, with the lemonade being followed by cocoa. During the interval, I conversed with my new acquaintances, who informed me what a rotten school Lonsdale's was all the while passing derogatory comments concerning the character of the food, which was really very nice. In a little corner of the lawn, obscured from the prying eyes of the more juvenile members of the throng, the Brigadier shook cocktails with a practised hand. These were accepted gratefully by the ladies present, and also by Uncle Will, who had made an unobtrusive arrival, and Russel, who, though having quit the water had not bothered to change.

Tea being over, a potato-race was instituted by the host and hostess for the little tots, though this soon died a natural death. But now it was growing late. Myfanwy and I bade the Brigadier and his lady adieu, not omitting to mention what a delightful afternoon we had spent.

Miss Ward stayed behind as Mrs. Sutherland Brown's guest. Aunt Lillian having departed long before, Myfanwy and I sank into the luxurious cushions of Uncle Will's car and as we drove swiftly back to Spencerwood. I reflected on the effect the party had on me. I realized that my desires and inclinations were all centered in a rural life at the farm. Cows, chickens, a swim in our cool green river after the toil and heat of the day, a supper of brown bannocks, cheese and honey: in other words the simple life is all that appeals to me.

Lightning Source UK Ltd.
Milton Keynes UK
UKHW020224240221
379240UK00010B/2113